Dolls in Canada

Dolls in Canada

Reflections of our heritage
Instructions for making them

Marion E. Hislop

BOARDWALK BOOKS
TORONTO · OXFORD

Editor: Kirk Howard
Manuscript Preparation (2ⁿᵈ edition): Barry Jowett
Printer: Best Book Manufacturers
Design: Scott Reid

Canadian Cataloguing in Publication Data

Hislop, Marion E. (Marion Eileen), 1925-
    Dolls in Canada: reflections of our heritage: instructions for making them

2ⁿᵈ ed.
ISBN 1-895681-15-4

1. Dolls — Canada. 2. Dollmaking. I. Title.

NK4894.C3H57 1997   745.592'21'0971   C97-932388-6

1 2 3 4 5 BJ 01 00 99 98 97

We acknowledge the support of the **Canada Council for the Arts** for our publishing program. We also acknowledge the support of the **Ontario Arts Council** and the **Book Publishing Industry Development Program** of the **Department of Canadian Heritage.**

Care has been taken to trace the ownership of copyright material used in this book. The author and the publisher welcome any information enabling them to rectify any references or credit in subsequent editions.

Printed and bound in Canada.

 Printed on recycled paper.

Boardwalk Books
8 Market Street
Suite 200
Toronto, Ontario, Canada
M5E 1M6

Boardwalk Books
73 Lime Walk
Headington, Oxford
England
OX3 7AD

Boardwalk Books
250 Sonwil Drive
Buffalo, NY
U.S.A. 14225

Author's Note:

The dolls reflect the time and place in which they were made. The dolls of today will one day reflect their own time and place in our heritage story. I want to express my sincere appreciation to all those, past and present, who have helped to bring this book into being. This is your book as well as mine. In particular I would like to thank Kirk Howard for his editorial work, and Barry Jowett for preparing the second edition.

Thank you each and every one.

MEH

Marion Hislop has had a life-long interest in dollmaking and collecting. This interest became public in 1977 when she put together her "Good Neighbour Doll Show" in order to entertain children in schools and public libraries. This hsow was made up of dolls both from the various regions of Canada and from the many cultural backgrounds which make up the Canadian mosaic. Because she believes that dolls are the storytellers of the people, through the "Show" she tried to increase understanding and tolerance.

Mrs. Hislop was born and educated in the city of Toronto. She now lives in Edmonton.

The author's mother, 1900

In loving memory of my husband, John Hislop

Contents

Mary Ann, a heritage rag doll

The Doll Lady

I want to introduce myself. My name is Marion Hislop, and because of my interest in collecting and making dolls, my family and friends call me "the Doll Lady."

I have been collecting dolls for many years now. Each doll is unique, and each doll tells a story. In fact, I believe that dolls are the storytellers of people and their heritage — and this book records some of these stories.

Later in the book, I will be showing you dolls from the many regions and cultures that make up Canada, and then I will show you how to make some dolls. But first, I want to tell you a story about myself and my love of dolls.

The story which I am going to share with you begins on a lovely bright December day in Black Creek Pioneer Village — a reconstructed nineteenth-century village on the outskirts of Toronto. I was visiting on this day because I was going to make a special doll for the village, and I needed to have very old materials with which to make it. I wanted this doll to look as though it were really over 100 years old, and that it had belonged to a little child who had lived in pioneer days.

I invite you to come along with me as I make my rounds. Of course, we must promise not to be in the way of the workers.

Our first stop is at the shop of the village weaver. As we open the door to his shop we see that Weaver is working at his loom. He is weaving colourful rags into floor mats. I explain to Weaver why I am there, and he shows me a barrel which stands behind the door to his shop. In the barrel we find pieces of old cloth and rags. While Weaver and I are sorting through the rags he tells me that he uses these pieces to weave the long strips to make the mats.

Our search is most successful, for we found the skirts from two old dresses, and these will make lovely dresses for the little rag doll. As Weaver helps me to gather up the rags and to return them to his old rag barrel, I see a little piece of plaid silk, and I ask him for this as well. I thank Weaver for his kindness, and also for the donations towards the little heritage doll.

Our next adventure will take us across the dirt road and along the wooden sidewalk to the home of Mr. and Mrs. MacKenzie. Mr. MacKenzie is the village clockmaker, while his wife does sewing and dressmaking for the people in Black Creek Village. As we enter the front door, we can see the old clockmaker working on a beautiful old clock. He does not seem to mind that we have stopped to watch him at his work. He tells us how he tries to make these old clocks work again. Mr. MacKenzie also tells us how he goes from house to house in the village to wind the clocks, as he does not like them to be wound by different people. He explains how clocks should not be over-wound, and he reminds us that in the days of Black

Mary Ann

Creek Village, there wasn't any electricity to run the clocks.

But now we must continue with our doll-materials-collection bee. Mr. MacKenzie tells us to go across the hall and on through the parlour to the warm kitchen, where we will find Mrs. MacKenzie at work at her little sewing machine. This sewing machine is operated by a treadle which Mrs. MacKenzie works with her foot.

Once again I explain why I am visiting the houses in the village today, and Mrs. MacKenzie invites me to sit down while she makes us a cup of tea. It does not take long to make the tea as the big old kettle has been singing away on the back of the big old wood-burning stove all morning.

While Mrs. MacKenzie and I are enjoying our tea, we sort over bits and pieces of trim and ribbons which are in a sewing basket. I pick out the things which I think will be useful for my doll. As Mrs. MacKenzie is returning her sewing basket to her shelf, she asks me if I would like to have some tiny white buttons. There is an old glass jar filled with all kinds of buttons, and I carefully choose some tiny white pearl buttons which I will sew onto the doll's underclothes. Soon I am again trying to express my thanks for these donations, and for the cup of hot tea.

Next we move on to the village inn. This inn is called "Half Way House." Many inns like this were called "Half Way House" because they were half way between one town or village and the next. In pioneer times, the roads between towns were very rough, sometimes no more than paths through the bush and around the creeks and ponds. On stage coach journeys, both passengers and horses needed frequent stops, and so these half way houses grew up. Here the passengers could have a meal, and the driver could change his team of horses. Some of these rest stops were only rough log shacks, while others were impressive two-storey buildings like this one in Black Creek Village.

In Half Way House, I see my friend Mrs. Baker who is busy setting the table for the noon dinner. She smiles at me, and willingly takes time from her work to help in my search for old materials. In a cupboard drawer Mrs. Baker finds a bit of old Irish lace and a linen cloth, neatly patched, as well as a long strand of linen cord. This linen cord was made from flax grown on the nearby farm. When the flax ripened, it was cut and dried in the sun. Then it was spun and wound into a large skein ready for use. I knew right away that I could use this cord to sew on the rag doll's head, and I was also sure that the head would never come off, for the linen cord was very, very strong. Mrs. Baker tells me that dinner will soon be served and suggests that we stay and enjoy some of the food which we could smell being cooked in the kitchen. While we are enjoying our meal, perhaps I could take a few minutes to tell you why I wanted to make this special little rag doll for Black Creek Village.

Before I began my collection bee that day, I had been doing quite a lot of researching so that I would know just what I would need in order to make this rag doll in just the same way she would have been made in the days before 1867. This doll was to look as though she had belonged to a child living in Black Creek Village at this time in our pioneer heritage.

Did you know that we have very few samples of the pioneer period in our museums? The reason for this is that the little dresses and suits were often passed on from one member of the family to the next in size, until the clothing was worn almost to rags. Another reason was that nothing was ever thrown away if there was a use for it. Rags and used clothing were made into all sorts of useful items for the family and the home. They were used in the making of quilts for the beds, rugs for the floors, as a wick for lamps, and were even at times wrapped around the feet for warmth when there were no shoes to wear. Newspapers and rags were stuffed around the doors and windows to help keep out the cold winds.

There were even men who came around looking for old rags to be used in the making of paper at the paper mills. These men were called rag-pickers, and the villagers were often glad for a little cash.

As a dollmaker, I am very glad that some of these old rags were used to make little rag dolls. Pioneer dollmakers were wise in the ways of "making-do," and so these rag dolls were usually one of a kind. Some dolls were not much more than a few scraps of cloth tied together into a doll form. It would often take the dollmaker quite a long time to save enough bits with which to make a doll. And these old rag dolls were sometimes the handwork of a young child who had worked away with a needle and thread, the results being rows of crooked stitchings and frayed ends. But I have no doubt that in the eyes of these young dollmakers, their dolls were more beautiful than any doll bought in a store.

For many children in pioneer days, a rag doll or even a wooden doll would be the only doll which they would own. These dolls were so well loved, and were played with so long that there was not much left of them to recognize as a doll. This is one of the main reasons why there are so few old rag dolls in our museums. And this is why I wanted to make this very special rag doll for Black Creek Village. She would be made in such a way that when visitors came, they would think she had always lived in the village.

Well, we have gotten off on a long story indeed, and now I think that we had better get on with our collection bee. Just before we leave Half Way House, we meet Mrs. Baker's friend, Mrs. Castle. Mrs. Baker has just been telling Mrs. Castle of our collection bee, and Mrs. Castle tells us that she will arrange for us to collect some nice fleece to use as stuffing for our little rag doll. Now, I wouldn't really have thought of going to the harnessmaker's shop for a bag of fleece, but Mrs. Castle has told us to go there.

The harnessmaker is busy repairing an old rocking-horse. It seems that this rockinghorse has seen many long years of rocking boys and girls, and is now badly in need of repairs. The young harnessmaker tells us that when he has completed these necessary repairs the little children of the village will enjoy many more years of rides. I think that the harnessmaker is rather enjoying himself, for working on the rocking-horse is fun, and a change from making harnesses and saddles and straps for the farmers and the people of the village.

The bag of fleece is soon packed and ready for me, but when I stoop over to pick it up I am surprised to find the strong smell of the barnyard is still on the fleece. Of course, I should have known this, but the harnessmaker is enjoying a good laugh on me. I guess he wonders how the Doll Lady could know so much about pioneer life, and not have realized that fleece would smell when it is first shorn from the sheep.

Mrs. Castle is on her way to meet me as I am leaving the harness shop. She too begins to laugh as I tell her of my experience with the fleece. Kind lady that she is, she tells me how to wash and prepare the fleece for use. We exchange our best wishes for a Merry Christmas as we say good-bye.

And so at last our doll-materials-collection bee is finished. But collecting was only the beginning. A dollmaking project must begin with a few preparations. So I decided to start with the fleece. It required many washes before it was clean. I then spread it out to dry, and when it was dry, I carded it. Carding means to comb the fleece back and forth, fluffing up the fibres, until all the bits of straw and burrs are removed. When the carding is completed, the fleece is soft and fluffy and it makes the best stuffing possible for a little rag doll.

Next all of the old fabrics, laces, and ribbons were carefully washed and pressed. The embroidery threads were selected, and spools of thread tested to be certain that they would not break. All the old buttons were then washed and sorted.

I did not wish to spoil any of these old materials by cutting them incorrectly or by not having the clothes fit the doll. So I decided that I needed to make a trial model first. Although my first doll has a little crooked nose, her eyes are bright and her smile is full of love. I named her "Molly Make-do." In the last part of this book, I will show you how to make a similar doll.

Almost a year after our doll-materials-collection bee, Mary Ann, our rag doll, was ready to go to Black Creek Village to live, a fine example of dolls from the nineteenth century. Her story is the story I've just told. And while she is a recently made doll, she does reflect the spirit of those pioneer times — in her clothes, in the materials from which she is made, and in the way in which she was made. In the following pages, you will meet some of Mary Ann's friends — many different kinds of dolls from many different parts of Canada, all of them telling you, in their own ways, Canada's story.

Dolls

Reflections of our Heritage

Canada is a diverse and large country. Some Canadians have lived here for many generations; some have just recently arrived. All of them have a rich heritage, and all of them have dolls which reflect that heritage. With Mary Ann and Molly by my side, let me introduce you to some of our friends.

I want to show you dolls that Canadian children have treasured for years. Your own dolls reflect not just your interests, but also the world around you. The dolls on the following pages reflect the time and place in which they were made. First we will meet some native and pioneer dolls. Then we will meet some dolls that newly arrived Canadians have brought with them, then some dolls from legends and stories. After that I will show you how dolls can take many shapes, and be made from many different materials. Finally, I will show you some beautiful dolls made by artists.

Heritage Dolls

Stump Doll

This is a reproduction of the type of doll which a good many children would have had in the earliest days of settlement, especially in those areas where there were many, many trees. The settlers had to clear the land in order to build a cabin and start farming. There would have been a great amount of brush and small branches that needed burning. Clearing the bush was back-breaking work. There is no doubt that a father would have been very tired at the end of his long day, and yet he would have taken time to make his child a doll, or some other plaything.

Perhaps while father was resting beside the outdoor fire, he would have reached for a small branch, and taking out his pocket knife or perhaps his hunting knife, begin to carve out the face of a doll in the surface of the bark. These doll faces would become dolls for the settler children. Sometimes arms of twigs would be added, such as those shown here, or the shape of arms may have been carved into the wood.

Mother may have had a few scraps of cloth for the clothes, but often the doll would be left just as it had been carved. This doll is dressed much as she would have been in the early 1800s in Upper Canada, back in the bush country.

Wood Penny Doll

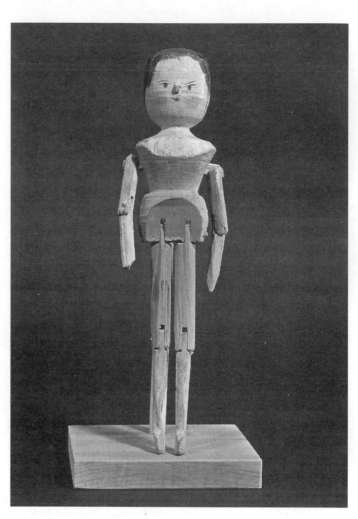

This prim little lady is a fine example of the wood penny doll. We see here the fine craftsmanship of our pioneer dollmakers. While the wood penny dolls were first made in Germany and in France, they were also made by the fathers and brothers of the settler families in North America.

The original wood pennies were sometimes crafted by an assembly line of wood craftsmen or craft families. Often only the heads and bodies would be carved in one house while the legs may have been worked on in another and the little arms made in still another. All of these little parts would at last arrive in one place and be joined together with the little pins or wooden pegs. Because the carvers had to do only one part, they soon became experienced and turned out a goodly number of parts in one day, and so these little dolls could be sold very cheaply. In fact, the large dolls were sold for a shilling in English money, and the smaller dolls were sold for a penny.

The dolls were probably very appealing because these were one of the first dolls at an affordable price that could move. Previously, dolls had been stiff jointed and could not be made to sit or have the arms moved about.

Step Dancing Doll

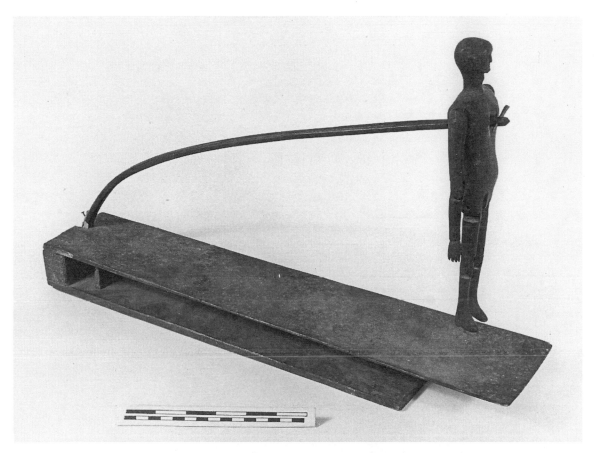

Step Dancing Dolls are part of the heritage of every province. Often these were made at home from a scrap of wood. Sometimes a travelling man would arrive in a village and would either sell these dolls or put on a little show and give the dolls in return for food and lodging. In the early days of Canada, work was often seasonal and when times were difficult and money scarce, people turned to giving services in return for a meal.

The method of making the doll dance was to tap the board. The vibrations made the doll dance.

The doll shown here was made in Quebec in the 1800s. I plan to show you how you can make a simple version of these wooden dolls in the next section of this book.

Iroquois Doll

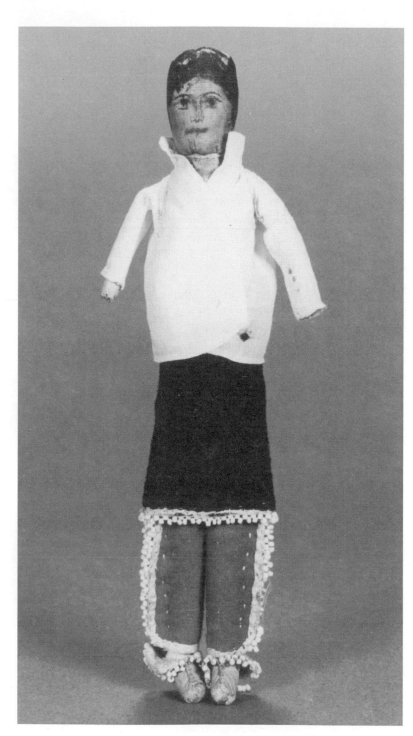

This doll was made by the Iroquois Indians in 1792, and is believed to be the one given by the Iroquois to the daughter of Sir John Graves Simcoe, the first Lieutenant-Governor of Upper Canada.

It has a cloth face and dress with bead-work leggings.

Two Old Rag Dolls

Here are two very early rag dolls from Ontario, made just like Mary Ann and Molly, our travelling companions. These dolls form part of the Percy Band Collection of nineteenth-century toys at Black Creek Pioneer Village.

The doll sitting is covered in cotton canvas, with painted features, hands, and feet. She is wearing a red serge dress and bonnet. Her friend is also a canvas and painted-face doll and she is wearing a natural-coloured flannel dress.

Old Couple in Rocking Chair

These are early dolls from Quebec. You can clearly see the detailed features. They are of stockinet fabric, with painted and stitch moulded faces. The great care taken with the faces and the hands gives the dear old couple life-like characteristics.

Sugar Bag Rag Doll

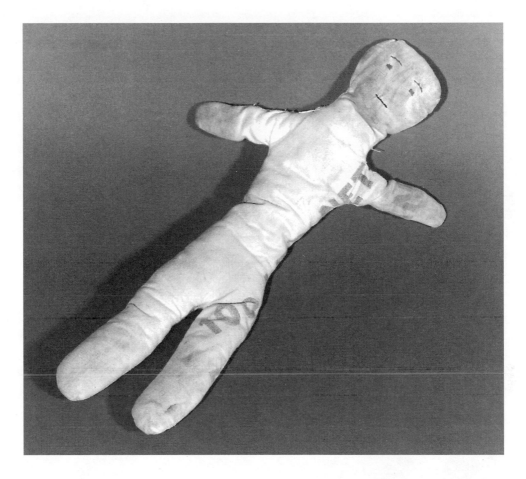

A child of the 1980s may not know much about sugar bags, but a child of the prairie homesteading days certainly would have. Sugar was generally delivered to the farm families in 50- or 100-pound bags. The empty bags were used to make tea towels, pillowcases, table cloths, underclothing, and, yes, even at times diapers for the baby. Many a girl or boy was sent off to school wearing clothing made from sugar bags.

This little doll is from the Manitoba Museum of Man and Nature. It is handmade from a sugar bag. "100 Bs. Net Granulated, Established 1854, Canada and Dominion" can be plainly seen on the doll's body. The doll is 43 cm long, and the face is embroidered in a simple chain stitch.

West Coast Indian Doll

This native doll is from Nass River, British Columbia. Many of the coastal Indian doll carvings were of a ceremonial nature. But I believe that this doll was intended for children to enjoy and play with. The doll is sitting in a woven grass swing. The face is of wood — look especially at the teeth. The hands are of wood, trimmed above the wrists with soft feathers.

Inuit Dolls from the Eastern Arctic

The people represented in these lovely doll figures are from Pangnirtung, Baffin Island. These dolls are almost life-size and about 50 years old. There has been great care taken with the detailed shaping of the facial features, and this gives the dolls such character.

The mother's hood is a carrying pouch for the baby and is part of the parka. Only the women wear this type of parka hood, and it would be lined with cleaned dry moss and would act as a disposable diaper for the baby. The clothing is made from seal and caribou skins and fur.

Inuit Dolls from the Western Arctic

These dolls are from Coppermine, North West Territories. The clothing is in the modern style, cloth with fur trim. The coming of the fur trader and the Hudson's Bay Company brought cloth to the native people.

Note the tattoo on the face of the grandmother. This is no longer the fashion with the Inuit, and the other dolls are not tattooed.

The nose of each doll has been very carefully shaped by rolling the cloth; it is then sewn to the doll's face. Father has a mustache, while the child is all but hidden by the parka. The footwear is leather with the uppers made from the blanket cloth.

Dolls from the Ukraine

These dolls reflect the heritage of our Ukrainian Canadian people. The fine hand work of the Ukrainian culture is known the world over. These handsome cloth dolls are dressed in colourful costumes.

The Shumka Dancers are a group of Ukrainian-Canadian dancers who perform all over the world. Here we see the young men dancing with a large Marena doll in a ceremony to celebrate the coming harvest. While the men are dancing, the young women are weaving wreaths. They then toss the wreaths into the stream, and, according to tradition, the young man who picks up the reath is destined to marry the young woman who wove it.

Japanese Cloth Doll

This little doll stands only 11 cm high. It is a silk-wrapped wire frame doll. The features are finely painted, and the hair and costume show the Japanese love of fine art. There is just a suggestion of tiny hands shown at the edge of the kimono sleeves. Every detail of the clothing is authentic including the obi sash.

Caribbean Doll

This doll was made in Jamaica around 1900. The doll is a laundress and her tray holds bags of laundry. Notice the money pocket, with the small buttonhole opening.

This dollmaker has taken great care with the smaller details of the doll. Look at the stitching to shape the toes which can be seen below her long skirt.

Dolls from Stories and Legends

Anne of Green Gables Doll

Perhaps the best known young woman from Canadian stories is Anne of Green Gables. She is the central character in a series of warm, beautifully written stories by Prince Edward Island writer Lucy Maud Montgomery. Anne Shirley is a young orphan girl who goes to live on a farm and the books are about the adventures and misadventures of this high-spirited girl growing up in P.E.I. in the early 1900s.

Raggedy Ann Doll

Perhaps the most famous rag doll is the Raggedy Ann Doll. Raggedy Ann and Raggedy Andy are dolls in stories written by Johnny Gruelle to entertain his young daughter. In these books the impish red-haired dolls come to life and have many exciting and mysterious adventures.

Raggedy Ann has become so much a part of the lives of children in the United States that the US pavilion at Expo 67 featured a huge and colourful display of them, part of which is seen above.

Evangeline Dolls

Here are two dolls from the Evangeline story. La Femme de Clare (on the left), an Acadian farm woman, is dressed in the style of the 1750s.

Evangeline (on the right) represents the E legend told about the Acadian people, at the time of their expulsion from the lands around the Bay of Fundy. When the poet, Henry Wadsworth Longfellow, was visiting friends in Nova Scotia, he overheard this story being told, and later turned the legend into a famous poem.

The poem tells how Evangeline had become separated from her fiancé at the time of the expulsion. Somehow Evangeline was rushed onto a ship, thinking her dear love was on the same ship. The ship had sailed by the time she discovered he was not there. Everyone assured her that she would catch up with him when the ships docked for supplies of food and fresh water. But she never did meet him. Each time she came to a port, she was told he had already been there. Evangeline spent the rest of her life looking for the man she hoped to marry.

One version of the legend says Evangeline went to a nunnery which cared for the sick. When she was an old woman, a very sick old man came in seeking care. Evangeline bent down, and lifted the man's head to give him a sip of water. She looked into his eyes and realized that this was her lost fiancé. But the man was already dead.

35

Little Red Riding Hood, and Grandmother, and the Wolf

This well-known story is a good one to show how versatile rag dolls can be. This one doll illustrates three characters out of the Little Red Riding Hood story.

First we see Little Red Riding Hood, and then, hiding under her skirt is — Grandmother. If we turn dear old Grandmother around, and carefully pull up her cap, we find the Wolf! Yes, there he is, with his big white teeth showing in a happy grin.

Tea Doll — a local legend

A Tea Doll? Yes.

This doll is stuffed with imported tea, and is very much a local folk story, specifically relating to the Indian community of North West River in Labrador. The Indians who live in this community are Montagnais and Naskapis who for centuries lived a nomadic life in search of caribou.

The story goes that many years ago a woman from North West River, named Mary Gregoire, was making a doll for her daughter, Rose. Since space and storage were always problems for people who were travelling constantly, Mary decided to stuff Rose's doll with loose tea. But Rose's uncle would raid the doll regularly and by winter's end the doll was quite floppy.

There has been a revival of interest in dollmaking in this part of Canada, and now tea dolls are made by a number of dollmakers in North West River. The tea doll shown here was made by Angela Andrew.

John Glasier's Woodsmen Dolls

These three New Brunswick woodsmen dolls are named for John Glasier, a strong and famous lumberjack who lived in New Brunswick in the nineteenth century. The dolls are about 31 cm high. They are stuffed with painted cotton faces. Notice the noses and the moustaches and long hair, and you will agree that these dolls are beautifully crafted.

From left to right: The first doll is wearing a hooded habitant-style coat with the voyageur sash. He has moccasins on his feet and woolen socks and mitts. The second and third dolls have wide belts, wool pants, and are both wearing sweaters, felt hats, and boots laced up the front.

Dolls from Different Materials

Cloth Cut-out Dolls

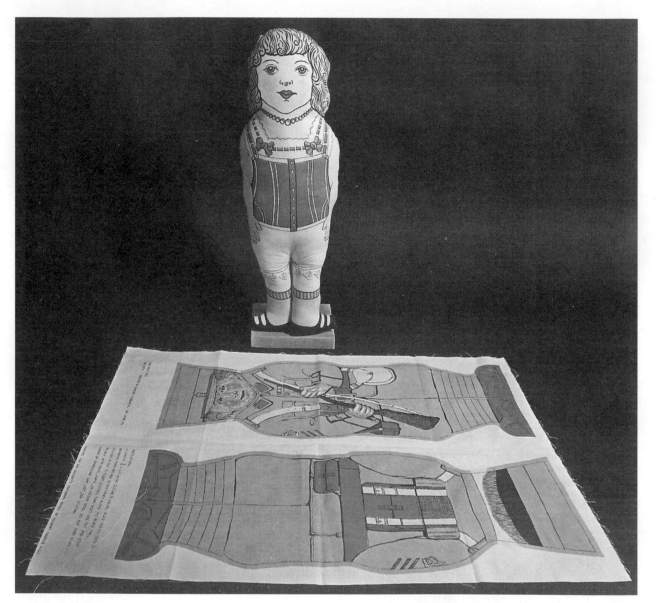

These dolls were designed and painted by an artist onto cloth, printed, and reproduced to be sold in fabric shops. Dollmakers would then need to cut and stitch these and stuff them with cotton batting.

The dolls shown here are reproductions of dolls painted by Samuel Finburch in 1915 — one is a young woman and one a British soldier in World War I.

China Head Doll

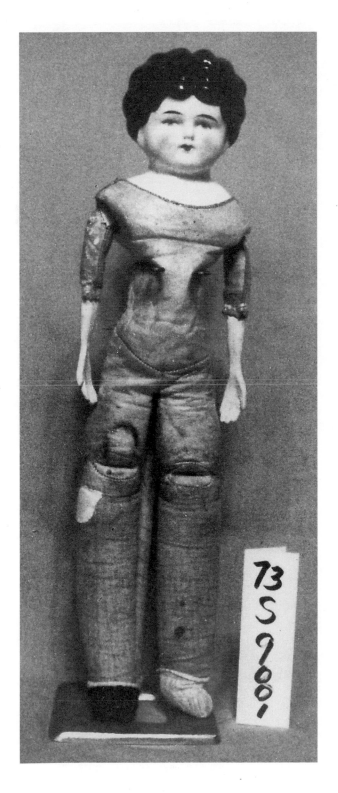

Here is an example of a doll popular in the late nineteenth century. A doll's head, made from china, was bought in a store or from a catalogue. Then it was up to the dollmaker to add the body. In this case a styled leather body has been added. Note the construction and the hinge for the knees. Notice as well the size of the legs in comparison to the slender arms, and the fine china hands.

Wax Doll Made for Queen Victoria

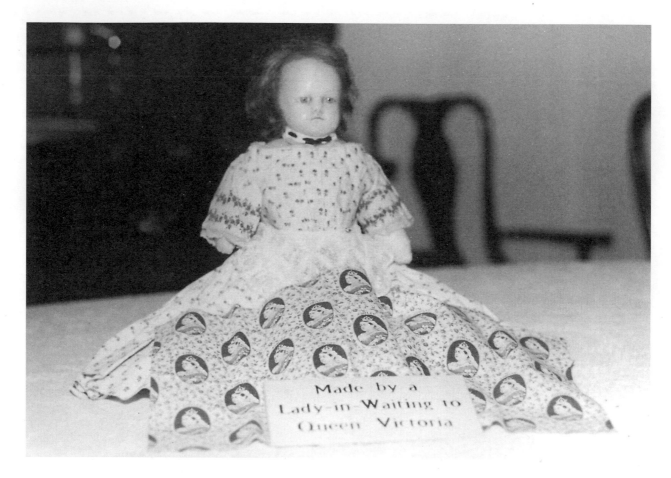

Made by a
Lady-in-Waiting to
Queen Victoria

Queen Victoria was known to have loved dolls. This old doll was made by one of her ladies-in-waiting. The head of the doll is wax, a fragile material. If it was too near the heat, it would melt; if left out in the cold, it would crack.

After Victoria became queen, wax dolls were made to look like her, and a few of these dolls can be found in museum collections today.

Celluloid Doll

Celluloid, an early type of plastic, was another material from which older dolls were made. This tiny doll in highland dress is only 8 cm tall, and came to Canada a long time ago from Scotland.

Chinese Pincushion Dolls

This pincushion was made in China. Each little doll on it has a white silk bead head, with a painted face. The bodies are made of satin, and each doll is reaching out and linking hands with the dolls on either side so that all the dolls together form a circle around the pincushion.

Worry Dolls

Have you ever lost a tooth, and then put it under your pillow for the tooth fairy to take away and leave a gift of perhaps a dime? Well, these worry dolls from Guatemala in Central America are like the tooth fairies. It is said that if we put our worries under our pillows at night, the worry dolls will come and take them away.

See the tiny bundles on the heads or backs of these little dolls? These are the worries which they are carrying away.

The dolls are only about 2.5 cm long. They are made by wrapping many coloured threads around a wire frame. The wire is bent at the ends to form the little feet.

Bedroom or Boudoir Doll

These dolls were placed on the pillow after the bedspread had been neatly pulled up, and were known as bedroom (or boudoir in French) dolls, or sometimes as Flapper Lady Dolls.

This doll is Madelaine. Her costume is called a "Yama-Yama" suit. It is made of black and white sateen cloth, and there are pom poms on the hat, jacket and the slippers.

The head is composition material, and painted; the hair is a mohair wig. The body is stuffed muslin. These dolls often have very fancy outfits and dresses, and some of them are as long as 137 cm, and would often be twisted into very grotesque shapes because of their long legs.

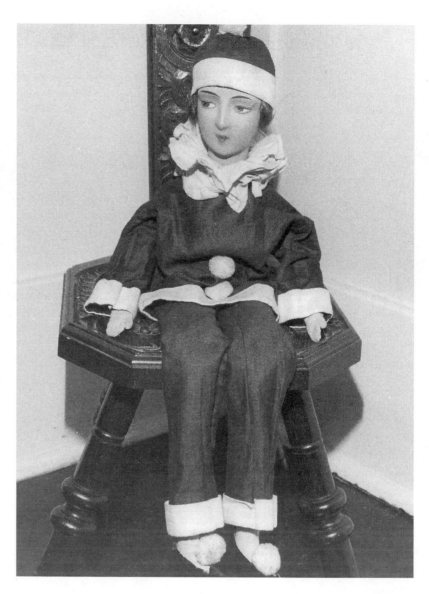

Russian Matroshka Dolls

These dolls from Russia are always made out of wood, and are always fascinating. Each doll fits inside the next bigger one, until, as in this case, all eleven dolls are inside the largest one.

Dolls by Artists
Dolls of John Halfyard
Dolls can be more than just play things — they can be works of art

John Halfyard was nearly 80 years old and almost blind when he began to make his dolls. The dolls in their own way tell the story of John and his hard life.

As a small boy he had been left with a circus, and the circus people brought him up. When he was a teenager, he left the circus and led a very independent life. But when he grew old and ill, hea was very lonely. Then he met Aileen Devereux. She invited John to come and live with her family.

Aileen is a fine artist. One day John was telling her about some of the adventures of his life, and all the time he was talking he was twisting some bits of cloth which Aileen was going to use in a

project, and had left beside John's chair. When Aileen saw what he was doing, she asked him if he thought that he could make doll figures from cloth, which would tell other people about his fascinating life. John never had much schooling, and by now he was not able to see to write, but he had al of these ideas in his head, about the different events and people that had been part of his life.

So John began to make dolls. He could see a little colour, and also shadows, and he chose his fabrics by the feel of the textures. His hands became the artist's brush and the doll were his canvas.

Each day before Aileen left for he studio, she would thread twenty or more needles for John. While the family was away all day, John sat and make his dolls. John was 94 years old when he died, and he left behind him a wonderful story as told by his beautiful dolls.

Dolls from Betsy Howard

Brittany

Betsy Howard was a gifted artist. She not only made beautifully crafted dolls, but she used her talents to bring delight and happiness to orphaned and homeless children who had suffered bitterly during World War II.

Betsy was careful to have her "little people," as she called them, correctly attired, and to have authentic and high quality materials. The hair was obtained from a local barber. Silk and velvets were used for the bodies, as well as skin-toned cottons. The faces were hand-painted in water colours, oils, or pastels.

Betsy died in 1950 and her dolls are now part of our heritage, on display at the museum in Courtenay, British Columbia.

50

Pirate

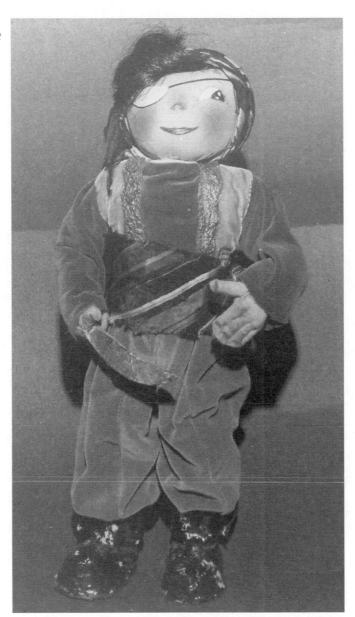

Brittany

This beautiful doll was named after her home province in northern France. Look at the clever way Betsy has created her little face. The wisp of hair over her forehead gives the idea that sweeping is hard work. Brittany is wearing clogs, and her dimpled knees are tinted pink. The fingers are almost life-like. And the desire to please is shown by the expression on her face.

Pirate

This doll delights us with his show of pride and impish bravery. Although he is carrying a sword, there is nothing to fear from this gallant lad. Don't you think that the eye patch shows us how this fine artist was able to create the small details which give her dolls such a realistic appearance?

Shelly Fowler's Pedlar Doll

Shelly Fowler is an artist who works in paints and soft sculpture. I have personally seen some of her soft sculptures and I felt compelled to touch them to see if they were really made from cloth. One tiny jug was so perfectly shaped it looked as though it had been made from clay.

This Pedlar Doll appeared in the Royal Ontario Museum's Year of the Child display in 1979. Pedlars used to be seen on the street corners of every major city, and dollmakers have been making their own versions for many years. This doll has a cloth face, hands, and feet. Look at all the miniature articles this Pedlar Doll has for sale.

Dolls from Line Desjardins

These dolls depict early life in Quebec. The heads are of a soft ceramic which is baked and hand-painted.

From left to right:

Le Conducteur de Carriole - This man would be much the same as the modern taxi driver today. Le Conducteur would drive a horse-drawn sleigh over the frozen lakes and rivers, and through the streets of old Quebec.

La Boulangare—the outdoor oven baker.

Le Queteux du Compagne—the travelling postman. This man would go from village to village carrying letters and news and messages in return for his meals and perhaps a night's lodging.

Eaton Beauty Doll

EATON'S BEAUTY

5A-113. The famous **EATON** Beauty Doll, which has long ago proved to be a wonder in doll values. Body is made of papier mache, very light and unbreakable, enamelled flesh color, fully jointed hip, knee, shoulder, elbow and even the wrists, the hands are perfectly shaped, jointed head that fits in socket, can be moved in any position, eyes that goes to sleep with real eye lashes, large wig with long curls. Head can easily be removed and another replaced. Dressed in frilled chemise with open half hose and bootees. Size 19½ inches tall. Price........... **1.00**

Larger sizes with parted wig tied with bow of ribbon.

Size 21 ins. tall. **2.00**
" 22½" " **3.00**
" 26 " " **4.50**

5A-114. Heads without wigs for **EATON** Beauty. Price.. **25c**

Wigs for heads.. **25c** (Dollar Size)

Reproduced here is part of a page from the 1911 Eaton's Catalogue showing the famous Eaton Beauty Doll. Reproductions of these dolls, so popular in the early part of this century, are now being made by Dorothy Churchill of Toronto.

Dolls of Wendy Gibbs

Wendy Gibbs is an artist living in Sydney, B.C. These dolls are based on the Salish Indians, a local tribe on Vancouver Island. The dolls, obviously toddlers, are 66 cm tall and have delicately painted faces on porcelain bisque heads. Their eyes are hand-blown glass beads and they have human hair. Their bodies are made of fabric with porcelain bisque hands, and they are dressed in sweaters with the Salish Cowichan knitting design.

Elizabeth Nind and Applecraft

Art and history are combined in this rendering of
Robert Harris's famous painting of the Fathers of
Confederation gathered at Quebec City in 1864.

Elizabeth Nind of Belleville, Ontario has created
many different tableaux using apple dolls. Each
figure has a dried apple head and a stuffed fabric
body.

Dolls

Instructions for Making Them

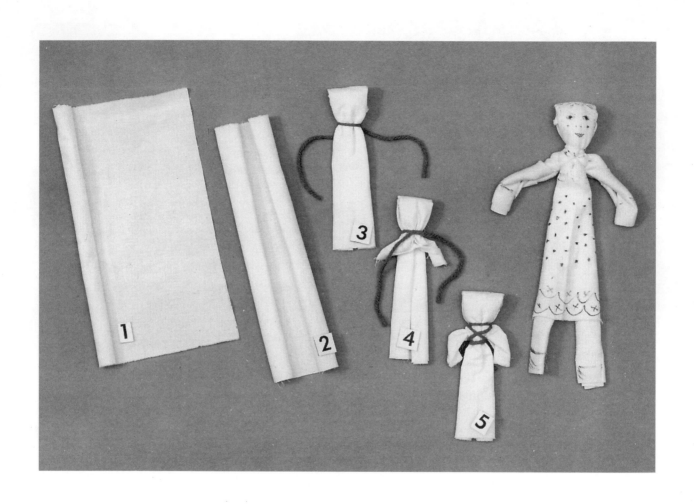

1 Rolled Rag Dolls

Also called Hanky Panky Dolls

This is a doll anyone will be able to make since it requires no sewing.

Materials Needed:
• 1 square of cloth about 35 cm long. Cotton cloth works best.
• 1 length of string or coloured yarn the same length of 35 cm.
• Scissors.
• Felt markers.

Method:
Follow the directions given below, and look at the examples in the photograph, working from left to right in the photo.

1. Cut a square of cloth to the size given above. Fold it in half and press the centre line with your nail firmly, so that the line will show when the cloth is opened flat. Unfold the cloth.
2. Roll the cloth from each side into the centre line as shown.
3. Turn the rolled cloth over so that the rolled sides are away from you. Fold down from the top about one third of the way. Now the rolls will be facing each other at the top. Hold this firmly in the left hand. (Lefthanded people reverse.)
4. Tie the string around the cloth which you have just folded over, and about half way down, the upper part will become the head. See photo. Wrap the string around several times, as shown. Tie a firm knot.
5. You will still have a little of the folded-over third below the head for the arms. Unroll the arms slightly and gently pull up the rolls, twisting them into position to form arms. Now wrap the string over the doll's body again, crossing at the waist. Bring the string under the arms and around the body. Tie a firm knot at the back. Stuff the head with bits of cloth, tissue, or stuffing, shaping as you work.

Your doll is now ready for you to draw on any facial features you may wish it to have. Add hands and feet if you wish.

For a boy: Cut the cloth between the rolls, or legs, about one third of the way up from the lower edge. The legs are now free.

For a girl: Cut out a piece from the centre between the rolls to form a skirt. Cut out a little square; then if you want the skirt shorter you can cut out more later.

Now There! You have made a doll!

2 Dolls made from cardboard tubes

The empty tubes from foil wrap or waxed paper and paper towels or toilet paper can be made into doll figures. These dolls can be used to make a Christmas nativity scene or other displays.

Materials Needed:
- Cardboard tubes of assorted sizes.
- White glue.
- Felt markers, a pencil, and a ruler.
- Scissors.
- Gift wrap paper, wallpaper, bits of cloth or felt.

Method:
1. Collect all of the materials needed and place these on a tray or in the lid of a box.
2. Cover the ends of the tubes. With the pencil, trace around the open end of the tube on the back of the wrapping paper. This makes a circle. Next draw a larger circle outside of the one just traced around the tube. It needs to be at least 6 cm larger in diameter than the first circle.
3. Cut this larger circle out. You will still have the smaller circle marked in the centre.
4. Now take the scissors and cut little slashes every centimetre or so into the outer circle.
5. Cover this outer ring with glue and fit this over the tube opening with the right side of the paper on top. Press down the sides to glue in place. This top will now become the top of whatever hat you decide to put on your doll.
6. Now lay the tube along the paper and measure the length of the tube. Mark it with the pencil.
7. Next, measure how much paper you will need by wrapping the paper around the tube and having a little bit overlap. Take the ruler and pencil and draw a line to the size you need to completely cover the tube.
8. Cut this marked paper out at the length you first marked, and then along the ruler line.
9. Carefully wrap the paper around the tube, and glue the overlapping edge down. Now the tube is covered.
10. Set the doll aside while you cut a piece of whatever colour you want for the skin of your doll. You need a piece 7.5 cm by the circumference of your tube. This you measure as you did above in 7.
11. Glue this face paper around the tube on top of the covered tube about 5 cm from the top. You can cut out bits of paper to make the features and glue these on, or you can use felt markers to draw them.
12. Using whatever paper you have chosen for the hat, cover the top part of the tube in the same manner, deciding how far down you want the hat to come over the face of the doll.
13. Now you must decide how you want to decorate your doll using the photo as a guide.

62

3 Apple Claus Dolls that you can eat

Materials Needed:
1 large red apple, 2 raisins, and 5 marshmallows for each doll.
• Toothpicks.
• 1 small paper drinking cup.
• A scrap of red paper or red felt.
• Cotton batting or stuffing.
• White glue.

Method:

1. Choose the best side of the apple to make the face.
2. Cut 1 marshmallow in half and cut one half in half again. Press these two quarters on to the apple for eyebrows. (They should hold, but if not, use a toothpick to hold them in place.)
3. From the other half of the marshmallow, cut a nose and beard. Press these in place using picks.
4. Push picks into the raisins and then press these in place below the brows.
5. Legs: Take 1 marshmallow and press a toothpick into it and place this at the bottom of the apple in front. Make another leg in the same way and place this beside the first leg. To hold the apple doll in place make a third leg and place this in back for balance.
6. Glue the red paper or felt around the sides of the paper cup and over the bottom. Glue a half marshmallow on the top. Glue the batting fur around the lower edge of the cup. Place the hat on Santa Claus using a pick at the back to hold it in place.
7. Set the doll on a paper doily or on a small plate.

These dolls make very nice place card holders for Christmas. Be sure to remove all toothpicks before eating!

4 Gumdrop Dolls

Materials Needed:
• Gumdrops, all one size for each doll.
• Wooden toothpicks.
• Paper umbrellas or plastic picks to add to decoration.

Method:

1. Body: Take one wooden toothpick and push one gumdrop down to the end of the pick, and then push another gumdrop down right on top of the first.
2. The face is made by turning a gumdrop on its side so that the large flat side is to the front of the doll and pushing this head gumdrop down on top of the two already there. Press all three gumdrops down so that they will not fall off.
3. Break one pick in half and push each half into a gumdrop about half way down the pick. Leave enough pick to hold the gumdrop in place when pushed into the lower part of the body. Do the same with the other pick and set these in place at the lower end of the body for legs. We like to use gumdrops all the same colour.
4. The arms are made in the same way, only place them at the sides of the upper body.
5. Now take a dark gumdrop and cut two small pieces for the eyes. Then cut a slice out of a red one for the mouth.

Using a sharp knife or a toothpick, cut out the spaces in the face gumdrop for the eyes and the mouth to go into. Dip the knife into very hot water and wet the cut-out places very carefully, but not the whole face. Now press the eyes and mouth in place using a toothpick to push them in fully. This activity needs to be carefully done so that the doll's face will look nice when completed.

6. The man's hat: We used about half of the black gumdrop from which we made the eyes, and used a whole toothpick to hold it in place on top of the head. We left enough toothpick showing so that anyone going to eat the doll will know that they must be careful to remove all of the picks first.
7. For the lady we added the umbrella with the handle pushed through one of the arms. A whole red gumdrop was her hat.

We placed our dolls on a paper doily. These little dolls make nice place cards party. Print the name of each guest on a small slip of paper, and set the doll in front of each guest at the party table.

Trace this shape onto cardboard

5 Baked Dough Dolls

These are not to be eaten!

Dough:
- 250 ml (millilitres) salt.
- 500 ml all purpose flour.
- 125 ml to 250 ml water to which a little dry instant coffee powder has been added and dissolved, approximately 4 ml.

Method:

1. Blend the salt and flour together with your hands and begin to add the water mixture *a little at a time*, mixing the dough to a stiff texture. Do not add too much water as the dough must be very stiff.

2. Turn dough out on a work table and knead the dough for about 5 minutes or until it is very smooth but does not crack.

3. Divide the dough in half and wrap one half in waxed paper while you work with the other half.

4. Place dough between two sheets of waxed paper and roll out flat with a rolling pin to .5 cm thickness.

5. Using a sharp cookie cutter, or a sharp knife and tracing around the pattern cut from cardboard, cut out the doll shapes.

6. Before removing the shapes cut in the dough, go all around them once again with the point of the sharp knife, and then remove all of the extra cuttings and bits of dough away from the cookies. Now remove the cookie cutters or patterns.

7. Using a flat knife blade carefully lift off the dough dolls and place them onto a cookie sheet which has been lined with foil wrap with the shiny side down.

   With a nail or pointed skewer make a hole at the top of the head. Make sure that the hole goes right through the dough. This will be used to thread a string through once the dolls are baked.

8. Draw on any designs and facial features you wish to have on your dolls with the point of a knife or a large pointed needle.

9. Bake the dolls in a 175 °C oven for approximately 40 minutes, or until the cookies are hard when tested with the flat blade of a knife. Remove pan from the oven when cookies are done. Allow cookies to cool completely *before* removing them from the pan.

10. Thread a coloured string through the hole at the top and decorate the dolls with tempera paints if you wish. Allow the paint to dry, and then for a nice glaze give them a coat of varnish. The varnish alone makes a very nice finish to the dolls.

Remember, these dolls are to be *seen*, not *eaten*.

6 Plastic Bottle and Sock Dolls

By using materials found in the home and a few supplies found in craft shops, you can make a very nice looking doll. These Bottle and Sock Dolls make handy doorstops or bookends or playthings.

There is almost no sewing to be done in making this type of doll.

Materials Needed:
1. Empty plastic bottle, such as a bleach bottle approximately one litre size. (A bottle without handles.)
2. One pair of men's socks, any colour.
3. A ball the size of a tennis ball. Or you can make a ball from crushed paper in a small plastic bag.
4. Glue-on eyes, sold in craft shops. Buttons or felt scraps can be used instead.
5. 5 pieces of coloured yarn cut to 30 cm each.
6. White glue.
7. Bits of red felt for a mouth.
8. A button for the nose.
9. Scissors.
10. A large-eyed darning needle.
11. Clean, dry sand or dry rice or beans to be used as weight in the bottle.

Method:
1. Wash the bottle and allow to dry.
2. Fill one-third of the bottle with the weight material of your choice.
3. Pull the sock up over the bottle, placing the toe of the sock at the bottom.
4. Smooth the sock up around the neck of the bottle, pulling up firmly.
5. Now cover the ball with a scrap of cloth or paper towel.
6. Place some glue around the neck of the bottle and at the lower end of the ball, and glue the ball in place, holding it down until it sits firmly.
7. Now carefully pull the sock top up tightly around the ball and tie a length of yarn around the gathered sock top. Leave some of the sock above the gathers free. Tie the yarn well.
8. The top of the sock above the yarn is the hair. Pull it neatly into shape.

9. Next, cut the ribbed top of the second sock off above the heel. Now cut the tube in half lengthwise, cutting through both thicknesses. These two pieces will be the arms.

10. At the back of the body, you will see that the heel is a bit lumpy. This is where we will place the arms. To make the arms, sew the two strips together at the cut ends so that you have one long sock strip with each end, having the finished edge of the ribbing showing. Centre the joined strip over the heel and pin in place.

11. Now thread the darning needle with yarn and push the needle into the centre, joining at the heel. Push the needle through it until you feel the bottle. Next, bring the needle back out through the sock in a different spot and through the arm strip so that when the yarn is pulled tight you will have two ends of yarn. Take out the needle and tie the yarn into a firm knot, and then in a bow.

12. Bring the arm ends to the front and sides of the body and pin in place. Sew the arms in place with the darning needle. Pull the little ends together and wrap a bit of yarn around them to make hands.

13. Place two good globs of glue on the sock face and apply the eyes in place.

14. Use a button or a bit of felt for the nose and mouth and glue these in place as well.

Your doll is now ready for you to decorate or dress up with a bit of trim or an apron, or perhaps you will want to add a wooden spoon tucked into one of the arms. We are sure that you will think of several ways to make your doll really special.

For a baby doll, you could use a white sock and a smaller bottle and ball.

These dolls would make a nice gift to give to someone special.

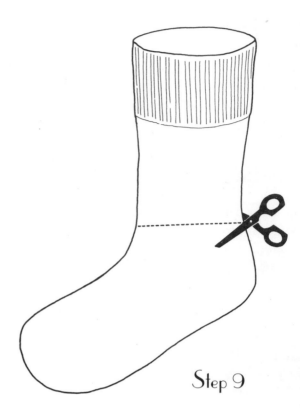

Step 9

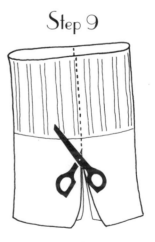

Step 9

70

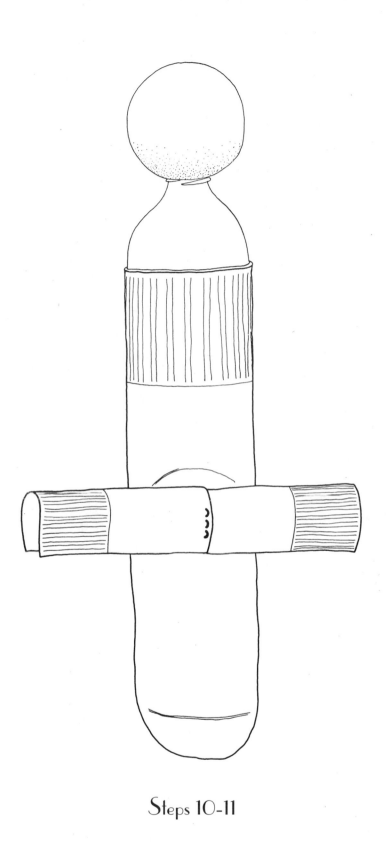

Steps 10-11

7 Clothespeg Dolls

Sewing terms and pattern pieces

1. To seam means to join two pieces of fabric together by placing the right sides (the sides of the material you want to show) together and sewing a row of stitching 1 cm from the raw edges of the fabric.
2. To hem means to turn up or turn in the raw edges and to sew this turned-in fold to the wrong side of the fabric.
3. To embroider, we use fancy stitches which help to define a pattern such as a flower (or in the case of dolls the face and other features), using embroidery thread.
4. To gather means to sew a row of small stitches along the raw edge of the fabric, usually at the top of the skirt of a dress or along the upper or lower edge of the sleeves of a dress. The thread should then be gently pulled. This bunches up the material, and makes it small enough to fit the opening of the piece of garment to which it is being sewn. It also makes the folds or bunches evenly divided all around.
5. The line drawings show samples of the stitches used in doll making.

   Running stitch is the one most often used in sewing a seam or to gather up the cloth.

   Hem stitch means to sew the hem or folded-over raw edges to the wrong side of the garment. Take tiny stitches through the fabric of the garment and through the hem by drawing the needle and thread through and over the hem fold while only showing tiny stitches on the right side of the garment. An outline stitch is used to define any solid line such as the eyebrows or lips. Satin stitching is placing the stitches so close together that they look solid. They are used to fill in the eyes and any place where you wish to show solid colour.

6. The bodice is the term used for the top of the dress above the waist and without the sleeves added. The bodice and skirt are sewn together in a seam after the skirt has been gathered to fit the waist or lower edge of the bodice.

running stitch

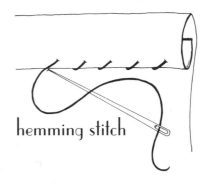

hemming stitch

gathering pulled up

Guide to Sewing

1. In making clothes for dolls it is important to press all of the fabrics before sewing them, as pressing is much harder to do after the small pieces have been sewn together. Pressing is a very important step in all sewing. Too often lack of pressing can spoil the end results of a sewing project.

2. When first learning to sew, it is helpful to try out the pieces you wish to make on a bit of used cloth, such as old bed sheeting or scraps of cloth, before starting to work on the fabric which you have chosen for the clothing you wish to make. While this may seem like a lot of extra work, you will be glad that you have taken this extra step once you have taught yourself to sew by this practice step.

3. Samples of Stitches used in Doll Making.
   a. Running Stitch
   b. Hemming Stitch
   c. Gathering pulled up
   d. Outline Stitch Embroidery (used for mouth and eyebrows)
   e. Satin Stitch Embroidery (used for the eyes and nose)

4. Using a sewing machine: *Do not use a sewing machine until someone who knows the machine has shown you how to use it!* A needle run through your finger is not a happy experience. *Care is the key word in all sewing and craft projects.*

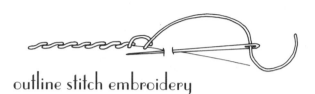

outline stitch embroidery

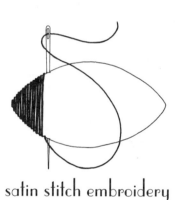

satin stitch embroidery

These symbols have been used in later drawings:

~~~~~~~~~~~~~~~~~~~~~   Stitch

\\\\\\\\\\\\\\\\\\\\\   Hem

ooooooooooooooooooo   Glue

-------------- ✂   Cut

— — — — — — — —   Fold

Simple method for cutting dresses and coats

I call this "The Double Fold Pattern." It can be used to make almost any type of coat or dress, including shirts, blouses, dress tops or bodices, as well as full dresses. This method can be used for almost any style by making simple adjustments when cutting.

To measure the size: Select the fabric you wish to use and lay the doll on it. Find how wide it needs to be so that the fabric will reach the hands and allow for small hems. Mark it on the fabric. If the doll's arms cannot be stretched out wide, then bring the fabric down along the arms to the hands. Mark this width with a pin or with chalk.

Next measure how long you want the dress or coat to be, once again allowing for the hem. Mark this length on the fabric. This length must be doubled so that when the fabric has been folded over you will have the correct length front and back from shoulder to hem.

Next fold the double-faced fabric over again from one side to the other so that you have half of the original width. (See diagram.)

You now have the two folds, or the double fold. The raw open edges are at one side and along the lower end. Before cutting the garment out you must allow for the seams. Measure the width of the body and add approximately 1.5 cm more for the seam.

To find out how wide you need to cut the sleeves, measure around the arm of the doll with a tape measure. To this measurement add 1.5 cm for the seam allowance, plus enough to give as much fullness to the sleeve as you wish to have. For example: 5 cm + 1.5 cm + 1.5 cm = 8 cm. Thus measuring from the shoulder or top fold we would need to allow a 4 cm depth to give us a sleeve 8 cm wide when opened out flat.

Mark these measurements on the double-folded fabric for the arms and the half body. You only need to mark half the width on the double-folded fabric for the body because when the fabric is opened up after you have cut out the pattern, the dress or coat will be the full body width.

To make dress and coat openings you only need to cut up the centre fold on one side of the fabric. If you use felt for the coats there will be no need to hem any raw edges. For the

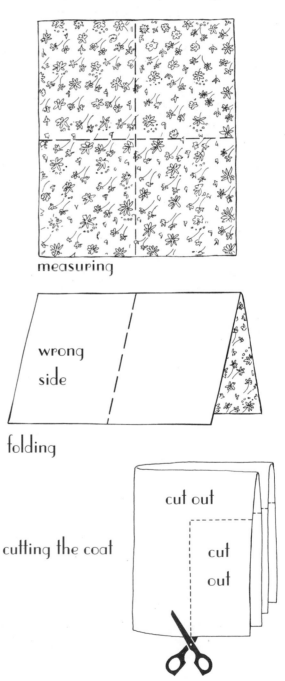

measuring

folding

wrong side

cutting the coat

cut out

cut out

75

neck openings, cut a very small slit along the top fold. It is always better to cut too little than too much, as you can always enlarge the opening after you try the clothing on the doll.

For dresses, you need to cut as well a vertical slit at the centre fold line so that the dress can be easily pulled over the doll's head.

You will need to sew very narrow hems all along the raw edges of the dress openings and neck edges. For dresses, it is usually best to place the cut at the back and in this way any extra width can be fitted under one side and the other side can be overlapped to cover it. You can either sew the dress onto the doll, as in the case of clothespeg dolls and apple dolls, or you can sew fasteners or buttons on the dress openings. For the coats, you may wish to leave the coat open.

To sew the dress or coat pieces together, make a narrow seam along the lower edges of the underarms and down the sides of the body. Always be sure to tie off your seams so that your stitching cannot unravel. Do this by repeating several stitches in the same place and tie a knot using the needle.

To make the dress full at the skirt, you can cut the cloth wider from below the waist than for the body measurement. Follow the outline drawings.

Fitting the dress on the doll:

Once the seams are completed, and all the hems sewn, and any lace or trim has been added, the next step is to fit the clothes on the doll. To do this, you can make little tucks or folds, or run a row of gathering stitches around the neck, or at the wrists or around the waist. These rows of gathers can be adjusted so that the fullness is evenly divided around the body. You may prefer to pull the extra material together at the back in a sort of a bustle or fullness. At the neck, a simple strip of lace sewn around a neck opening and then gathered, makes a lovely ruffle. The same can be done at the sleeve tops or at the wrist openings.

In coats, a little pleat can be made at the centre back and tiny buttons sewn over this. Coat tails can be cut and shaped, and the

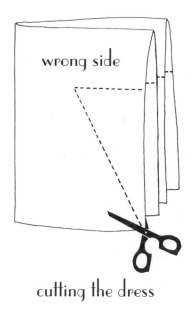

cutting the dress

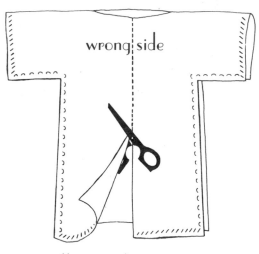

cutting coat opening

fronts can be cut shorter as we have done with some of our clothespeg men.

We know that after a little practice you will be designing all sorts of lovely outfits for your dolls.

A simple method for making pants

By following the drawings step by step, you will be able to make pants to fit most dolls.

Method:

1. Measure the width around the doll's body and double the measurement.
2. Add another 2.5 cm to the width for seam allowance.
3. Measure down from the waist to the length you wish — that is, to below the knee, or to the top of the foot.
4. Again add 1.5 cm for the lower hem, and 3 cm for the top hem or heading.
5. After marking all measurements, cut fabric to this size.
6. Fold fabric in half lengthwise with the right sides together and make a narrow seam along the open edges opposite the long fold as shown.
7. Make and sew a narrow hem at the lower edge, approximately 1.5 cm and a wider hem along the top at the waist approximately 3 cm deep.

Note: For this top hem, leave about 2.5 cm of the hem open if you are going to insert elastic.

8. The next step is to divide for the leg openings. To do this, measure the doll's inside leg (from the seat down) and add .5 cm to that measurement for a hem.
9. Now draw a vertical straight line right up the centre of the material, from the bottom up. The length of that line is the leg (plus hem) measurement.
10. At the top of that centre line, mark an "x".
11. Now measure .5 cm up from the "x" and draw a short horizontal line to points equidistant from the "x". (See diagram.) The length of that horizontal line depends upon the thickness of the doll's legs.

12. From the two ends of the horizontal line, draw straight lines down to the bottom, parallel to the centre line. You should now see a fat upside-down letter "u", which is really the pants.

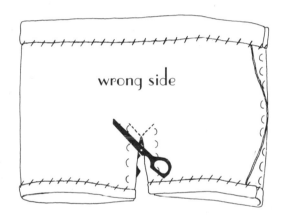

wrong side

13. Stitch along these two lines and the top horizontal line.
14. Very carefully, make a cut between this narrow seaming, being sure to keep the seams evenly divided and not to cut through the stitching. Then make two very small diagonal cuts from the "x" to just below the corner points. Do not cut the stitching. (See diagram.)

    It is necessary to be careful when doing this, but should the seams not hold, or should the material fray, run a second row of stitches over the raw edge and seam line. These are called overcast stitches.
15. Turn pants right side out and press if needed.

For Lady Dolls:

When sewing the top hem leave a small space unsewn for an opening so that you will be able to thread elastic through the top of the pants.

For Men and Boy Dolls:

Fit the pants on the doll and if there is any extra fullness or width pull this to the back and make a fold at the centre back. With thread to match the fabric, sew the fold flat to the pants taking very small stitches. Adjust the pants around the waist.

After reading all of the above instructions it may seem to you that this is a lot of work. It isn't. However, it might be best for you to make a few pairs of practice pants until you fully understand the method. Once you feel comfortable making pants this way, you will be able to make pants for almost every type of doll. Just be sure to get the width and length measurements correct, and to carefully measure enough length for the legs. I am sure that you will not have any trouble. It is very important to allow enough material from the waist to the top of the leg slit so as to have the pants cover the lower part of the body or the seat of the doll. I found this out too late more than once and had to make another pair of pants.

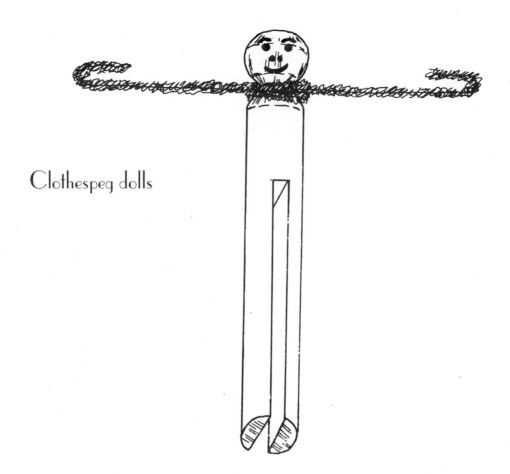

Clothespeg dolls

I used this type of pin or peg to hold the washing to the clothesline when I was a little girl. Dolls have been made from wooden clothespegs for a very long time. Perhaps your great-grandmother made this type of doll when she was a girl.

From the examples shown in the photographs and by following the instructions given here, you too will be able to make clothespeg dolls.

Materials Needed:
1. Wooden clothespegs that have two little legs. These are sold in craft supply shops. Some shops also sell wooden stands for the clothespeg dolls.
2. Fine felt markers.
3. Pipecleaners. (Sold in drug stores and tobacco shops).
4. Strands of embroidery cotton for hair, or wool or yarn, or if you want to make an old man or lady doll use white batting or stuffing. Paints may also be used.
5. Squares of coloured felt. (Sold in fabric and craft shops.)
6. Sewing needles and thread to match fabrics.
7. Scraps of dress fabric, and an assortment of lace or trim, as well as small buttons or beads.
8. White glue.
9. Scissors, and dressmaker pins.
10. A long knitting needle is helpful to help turn tiny things right side out.
11. Clear nail polish. (Optional)

Method:
Children between the ages of 4 and 11 can quite easily make these dolls using this simple method.
1. Gather all of the materials needed as shown on the previous page. For the simple method a sewing needle and thread will not be needed.

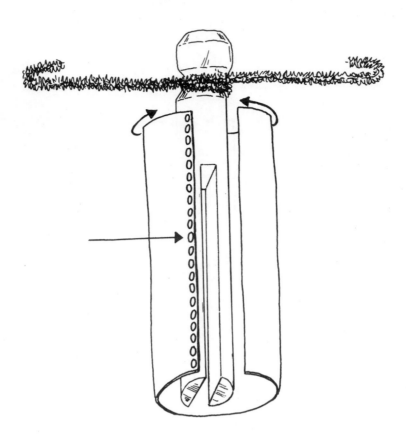

2. The clothespegs sold in craft shops are usually cut ready for doll making. (The feet have been cut off.)
3. Using fine felt markers draw a little face on the rounded side of the peg head, but be sure to keep the slit in the lower part of the peg in the centre so that the face will be on the front of the doll, and not on the side of the doll's head.
4. Wrap a pipe cleaner around the peg below the head and bring the "arms" completely around.

Dresses:

5. Choose a piece of cloth and cut a square 7.5 cm in size. This will fit around the peg from the arms down, leaving a little peg showing for the feet.
6. With the right side laying face down on the work table, rub glue along one end of the cloth. Make sure to have the glue come right to the ends.
7. Right below the arms, lay the clothespeg along this glued end and press the cloth firmly to the peg.

8. Carefully wrap the cloth around the peg until you come almost to the other end. Again rub glue along this edge and glue the cloth down over the peg. Hold in place until you are sure that the glue is going to hold.
9. Make a sash or belt by wrapping a narrow ribbon or a piece of coloured yarn around the waist of the doll and tie it in a bow at the back.
10. Hair can be made in several ways, by drawing it on with felt markers or paints, or by gluing on a bit of white stuffing or batting.
11. A simple hat can be made from a small circle cut from felt and glued to the doll's head.

Add some little item such as a tiny broom or a basket to your peg doll to make it look more interesting. Steps 5 to 10 above have been for a doll wearing a dress. If you wish to have your doll dressed in pants and a shirt follow the steps through to the end of number 4:

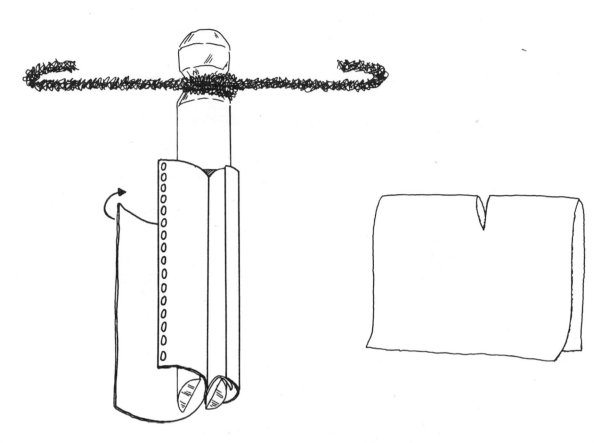

Pants:

5a. Cut two squares from coloured felt 5 cm in size.

6a. Keeping the edges even, carefully push the two squares of felt up through the slit in the peg, or the legs of the peg doll, being sure to push the felt all the way up to the top of the slit.

7a. Taking one square, place a little glue on the inside vertical edge and press down on the leg of the peg. Wrap the felt around the leg and glue into place. Do the same with the second square of felt. Hold the glued pant legs until the glue has time to take hold.

Shirt:

8a. Cut a bit of cloth 7 cm by 10.5 cm. Fold cloth in half so that the fold is along the top and you have two rectangles of cloth 7 cm by 5.25 cm. Lay the peg doll on this cloth so that the arms are lying right on the fold, and make a pencil mark on the cloth at the centre for the neck opening. Cut the folded cloth at this mark, making a small slit just large enough to allow the head to pass through.

9a. Open the cloth shirt out and with the right side facing up, place the shirt on the doll over the head.

10a. Wrap a narrow strip of cloth or a piece of string around the waist of the doll and tie a firm knot. Adjust the shirt around the doll's body so that it looks neat.

Hats:

11a. For a pirate hat, cut two small triangles from felt. Glue along all of the outside edges and place the peg doll's head between the two triangles. Press the triangles together, keeping the edges even and gluing the hat to the doll's head at the same time. For a soldier's hat, glue a black puff ball to the top of the peg and draw a strap under the chin on the face of the peg doll with a black marker.

By adding a little plastic toothpick your pirate or soldier will have a very nice looking sword to tuck into his waistband.

8 Clothespeg Dolls — advanced method

Clothespeg Dolls Dressed in the Fashions of the 1890s

The lady is dressed in dark green velvet with lace trim at the neck and at the wrists. She is wearing a green felt hat with a turned up brim and a tiny black feather sewn to the side.

The gentleman is wearing a black felt suit, a lace cravat or ruffle at the neck and a tiny bit of lace at the wrists. Under his tailcoat, he is wearing a red vest. His tall black hat and cane give him a fine appearance as he offers his arm to the lady.

Method:
1. Saw off the little points of the pegs or feet if this was not done before. Be sure to ask an adult who has used a saw before to help you the first time.
2. Smooth the wooden peg head with a bit of sandpaper. Line up the face with the slit in the peg legs and using felt markers, make the face. Allow this to dry and then coat it with clear nail polish if you want a sheen to the face.
3. Choose yarn or embroidery floss for the hair. Place a dob of glue on the top of the peg and at the back of the head. Starting from the side, carefully wind the thread around the head, making sure that the strands are very close together and making the circles smaller until you get to the very centre of the back of the head. Cut off any leftover thread and press the ends flat to the head. Allow to dry before going ahead with the next step.
4. Wrap a pipe cleaner around the peg below the head, crossing it over in back so that you have two arms. Bend the arm ends to form hands. These can be left like this, or covered with nylon stocking strips or felt.

Glue or sew these in place.
5. Cut a small piece of dress fabric 4 cm by 8 cm and with the right side facing up fold in half, with the fold along the top. This will give you a square 4 cm in size. At the centre of the fold make a small cut just large enough so that the doll's head will pass through the opening. Place this over the doll's head and fit it over the pipe cleaner shoulders and take two or three small stitches at each side to help hold it in place.
6. For the sleeves, cut two pieces of fabric 4.5 cm square. Take one piece and fold it in half with the right sides facing. Sew a narrow seam along one side joining the square into a little tube open at each end. Turn the tube right side out. Turn in a small hem at both ends of the tube through this hem using the running or gathering stitch.

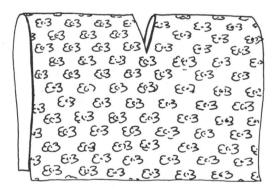

step 5

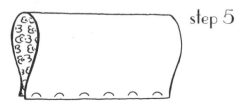

step 5

Leave the needle threaded in each end, which means that you will need to use two needles. Place the sleeve tube with the needles still in it on the arm of the doll. Fit into place at the shoulder and pull up the gathering thread to fit and tie off and knot thread and cut off the needle. Do the same thing at the wrist opening, adjusting the gathers neatly around the wrist. Do the same thing to make and fit the second sleeve. Take a few stitches at the top of the sleeves and right through into the dress top or bodice. If the dress bodice looks a bit messy at the shoulders, you can cover it later after the skirt has been completed with a "V" of lace from the waist and up over the shoulders to the back bringing it down into another "V" and sewing to the dress by taking a few tiny stitches. If you want to have a ruffle of lace at the wrist, wrap a bit of lace around the pipe cleaner arm before placing the sleeves on the doll.

7. For the skirt, cut a rectangle 17 cm wide by 9 cm deep. Fold this in half with the right sides together and with the 9 cm ends evenly together making a rectangle 8.5 cm by 9 cm. Sew a narrow seam along the 9 cm end of the rectangle. This will be the centre back seam of the skirt. Turn skirt right side out. Turn up a narrow hem at the bottom of the skirt and stitch to the inside taking very small stitches so that the right side of the hem will be neat. Next make a row of gathering along the top raw edge of the skirt, leaving the needle threaded as you did for the sleeves, place the skirt on the doll, bringing the skirt gathering up over the bodice, and pull up the gathering to fit the waist. Take a few stitches to secure the gather-threads and tie a knot and cut off the needle. Be sure that the centre back seam is at the centre back of the doll's body. You may now add the "V" of lace.

8. Your clothespeg doll is almost complete. Now you can make the hat. Cut a strip of felt in a colour to match the dress, 1.5 cm by 10 cm. Using thread to match the felt, roll this strip rather tightly with the 1.5 cm edge as the height of the hat. This will make a little solid tube. Sew a few stitches back and forth through all thicknesses to hold the felt tube together. Leaving the needle threaded, set this aside while you cut the brim. Cut a circle from the felt, 3 cm in diameter. Place the felt tube in the centre of the brim and sew the top of the hat and the brim together, working the needle up and down through the brim and along the lower edge of the hat top, and then fasten the thread off. This can be used just as it is, or a bit of trim can be added. We have placed a tiny bit of feather beside the brim and sewn both the feather and the brim to the side of the hat. Place a good amount of glue on the doll's head and set the hat in place. Press down well and hold in place for a few moments. Allow glue to dry before touching the doll again.

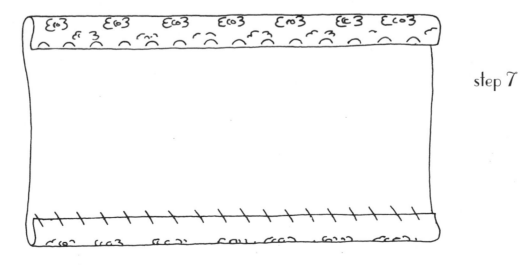

step 7

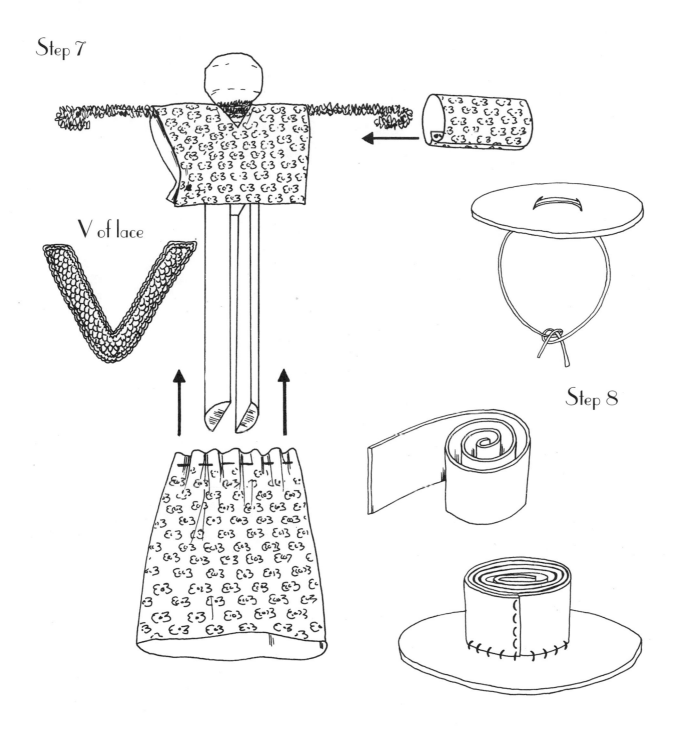

V of lace

Step 8

9. Place the doll in the round stand. You may glue it in place.

From the directions given for lady dolls, it will be quite easy for you to make other clothespeg dolls. I am showing samples of both male and female dolls from the very simple to make type to the more advanced method.

To make men follow the same steps as for the lady for the body, making the hair suitable for a man. The pants and trousers are made from tubes much like the sleeves for the dresses. I use mostly felt for our men as this does not need to be hemmed, and can be glued instead of sewn if you wish to do so. Cravats or collars are made from a piece of lace folded and gathered to fit around the neck of the doll.

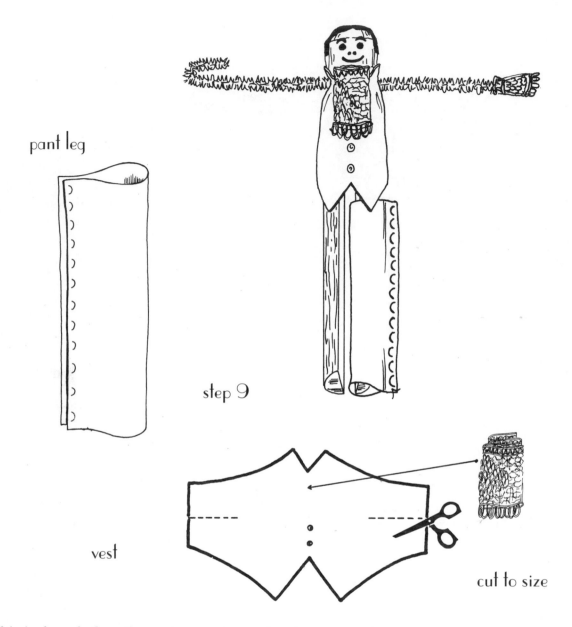

pant leg

step 9

vest

cut to size

This is done before the vest or coat are placed on the doll. To have a cuff showing at the wrist simply wrap a bit of lace around the pipecleaner arms and fasten in place with a few small stitches. The vest is cut in one piece as shown in the drawing. The coats are also cut in one piece following the double fold method shown earlier. In sewing the clothing for men we usually make very narrow seams on the outside or right side of the clothing as this makes fitting easier and neat. I place the pant leg seams on the outside of the peg legs.

86

Multicultural Clothespeg Dolls

I have made and added this collection of clothespeg dolls to my "Good Neighbour Doll Show."

In this photograph we see from left to right in the back row, a RCMP officer next to the Canadian flag; a Drummer Boy from the British Militia in the nineteenth century; a Bread Baker from the Gaspé Peninsula in Quebec; a Weaver from Wales; and a young Sweeper from Ireland.

On the next row from left to right, we find a Cheese Lady from Scandinavia; a Butter Churner from Estonia; a Guitar Player from Chile; a Dancer from Spain; a Basket Lady from Vietnam; and a Pearlie Man from England.

To the Doll Lady, the Pearlie Man represents an interesting part of English folk history. At one time, there were pedlars who went about the market places and streets of London, England, selling buttons made of pearl or mother-of-pearl. This comes from the pearly lining found on the inside of some shells, not the pearl used as jewellery. Some of these pedlars started to sew the pearl buttons on their hats and clothes and there began a custom until many of the button sellers would try to outshine their fellow button pedlars and started sewing the pearl buttons in all sorts of designs. Soon whole families would be all dressed in clothing covered with hundreds of pearl buttons worked into lovely patterns. While the pearlies no longer sell their wares, they still dress up in the pearly clothes on special days and at the fairs in and around London. So now these pearlies are a traditional sight to the delight of Old London visitors.

9 Kitchen Witch

The Kitchen Witch is said to bring good luck to both the cook and visitors to the household kitchen. I believe that luck, good or bad, is mostly of our own making. However, to hang a little witch doll in our kitchen, the central room of most Canadian homes, can add a touch of youthful spirit and pleasure to all who enter it. My own memories of childhood recall me back to the days when to come home from school to the warm kitchen was a pleasure looked forward to on cold winter days. Our old kitchen had a big monster of an old black coal and wood burning stove. There we roasted our feet, enjoyed big cups of homemade soup and ate cookies hot from the oven. The parlour or livingroom was hardly ever used in our house for everyone came to our back door and sat in the kitchen to visit. The sewing machine was always set up and grandmother usually held a sewing needle in her work worn hands. I remember my little sister and brother taking turns sitting on the treadle while one of the older children gave them a ride. To visit that old kitchen was a joy to every child in the neighbourhood. You could say our kitchen witch was our grandmother, for she surely could spin a tale of magic. But enough. Here is the way to make one for your kitchen.

Materials Needed:
1. 1 old nylon stocking. Also black felt and fabric for a dress.
2. A few bits of yarn in black and also in grey.
3. Polyester stuffing or cotton batting.
4. Thread - black, red, and colours to match the nylon and the dress fabrics.
5. Glue-on eyes. (I used 4 mm size.)
6. White glue.

7. A stick or a piece of dowel, or a pipe cleaner, or something to use as a broom stick.

Method:
Material for the broom straws; brown paper, or corn husks.
1. Cut the nylon stocking into a tube 15 cm in length. It will be open top and bottom.

Steps 1-6

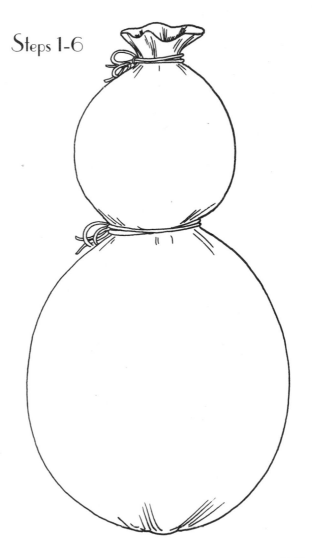

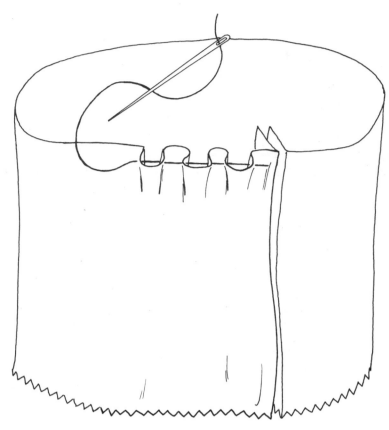

2. Sew a seam through both thicknesses at one end of the tube and pull the threads up tightly to gather the nylon tube closed, and fasten threads off well.

3. Turn the tube inside out and begin to stuff it with the polyester stuffing until you have the shape and body fullness that you wish to make.

4. Now gather the top end of the tube in the same way as you did at the lower end, only this time the gathered seam will be on the outside. You should have a fat rolled shape.

5. Next, tie a length of strong string around the tube about 1/3 of the way down from the top. This will be the head of your witch doll.

6. Turn the head so that the gathers and any folds are at the back and the front is smooth for the face of the doll. Thread a needle with thread to match the colour of the doll's nylon body. Working from the back of the head, push the needle through to the front to the place where you wish the nose to be. Taking very small stitches and pulling the work through to the back each time, mould and shape the nose to your liking. This is called soft sculpturing. After fastening off the nose thread, do the same work to pull in little sockets for the eyes. Do not glue the eyes in place until after your doll is completed.

7. The skirt or dress is made in one piece. Cut a strip of printed cotton 30 cm by 11.5 cm, using a pair of pinking shears, (scissors which have a zigzag edge). Otherwise, use regular scissors and leave the raw edges. Fold over so that right sides are together, and sew a seam along the two short ends to make a tube, (11.5 cm). Turn right side out. Sew a row of gathering stitches along the top about 1 cm from the edge.Leave the needle threaded and place the dress tube on the body of the doll. Cover the string tied around the neck. Pull up the

step 8

step 9

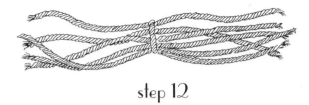

step 12

gathers around the neck and tie the thread off. The skirt dress should cover the body using the measurements given here. If your doll should be longer, then cut the dress the depth needed to hide completely the body.

8. Cut two hands from felt approximately 2 cm by 4 cm, in the shape of a mitt. Join the hands together, leaving the wrists open. Using an overcast stitch, sew the two hands starting at the wrist edge nearest the thumbs. Sew around the thumbs and then set the hands aside leaving the needle and the thread in the cloth until you make the broom.

9. For the handle of the broom, you will need a very narrow stick or dowel, or a pipe cleaner, which is what I used in the photograph. Cut the handle to about 15 cm and then make the broom straw from brown paper cut in strips. Corn husks or broom straws may be used. If you use corn husks, soak them in water first to make sure they are easy to work with. Wrap the broom strips around the handle at one end and then wrap strong thread around this several times. Tie firmly in place. A little clear nail polish painted over the string will help keep it firmly in place when dry.

10. Now return to the hands. Insert the broom handle between the hands with the handle at the top. Continue the overcast stitching around the hands and take a few stitches into or around the handle of the broom. When you have completed sewing the hands to the wrist opening, fasten your thread off.

11. Now pin each side of the wrist to the dress, making a small tuck or pleat between them so that the broom will fit into the body a bit. Using thread matching the dress, sew the wrists and hands to the dress. Continue sewing with the same coloured thread, fastening the broom handle to the doll's

91

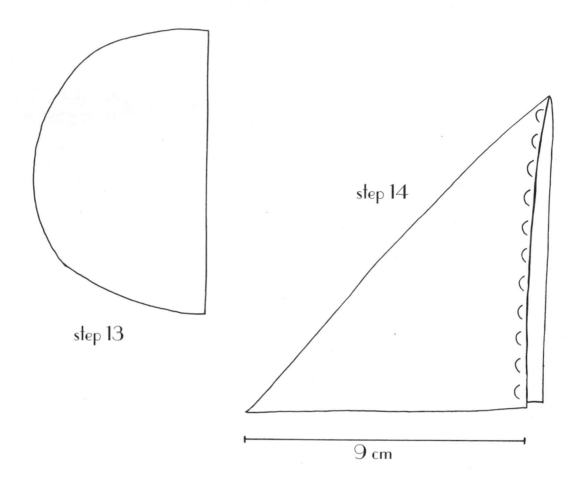

step 13

step 14

9 cm

dress. Adjust the broom so that it is placed evenly at the top and below the hands.

12. Cut a few strands of grey yarn approximately 18 cm in length and, bunching them together at the centre, sew them to the top of the doll's head so that once the hat is on the doll the hair will hang down on each side of the face but in a rather untidy way.

13. From black felt, cut a small cape to fit over the shoulders of the doll as shown in the drawing, however, you will need to measure the width around the doll's neck, and cut the cape to fit. As this is a soft sculptured doll our measurements are only approximate; no two dolls will be quite the same size. Place the cape on the doll, and sew the two points together below the chin of the doll.

14. For the hat, cut a 9 cm square from black felt. Fold it once diagonally to make a triangle. Stitch one side making a narrow seam. Turn the hat right side out. The hat is now pointed at the top and has a long pointed peak. Place the hat on the doll's head with the seam up the back and having the hat pulled well down at the front so that it covers the hair. Pull the back of the hat down over the top edge of the cape and with black thread, stitch the two together. Stitch the hat at the front to the head, and also take a few small stitches on each side of the head, being sure to fasten threads off well. Adjust the strands of hair about the face.

15. Using black yarn and a large-eyed needle, make a loop at the back of the head where the hat joins the cape. To do this push the needle through the cape and pull it right through, leaving a length of yarn long enough to tie into a large loop. Bring the ends of the yarn together and tie a firm

knot. Cut off the remaining ends. This loop is how your kitchen witch will hang up. The kitchen window is a nice place to display your witch doll.

16. The last thing to be done before you can say that our doll is completed is to sew a mouth on with a needle and red thread, and to glue the eyes in place. Allow the glue to dry before hanging up your kitchen witch doll.

10 Dolls built around
a wire frame or armature

The Apple Head dolls and Nut Head dolls (walnuts, filberts, or pecans are best), are most often made with a wire frame body. The method of construction is the same for each type of doll.

Materials Needed:
1. Fine wire, approximately 38 cm to 46 cm in length, two pieces for each doll.
2. Polyester stuffing or cotton batting.
3. Fabric or nylon stocking to wrap the body frame.
4. Sewing needles and thread to match body fabrics, and the clothing fabrics for the finished dolls.
5. Masking tape.
6. White glue.
7. Glue-on eyes or beads, for Nut Heads and soft sculpture dolls, dressmaker pins for apple dolls.
8. Yarn or wool for hair (or scraps of fun fur, and even human hair can be used).
9. The doll head: apple, nut or purchased doll head, or a soft sculptured head added to the frame.

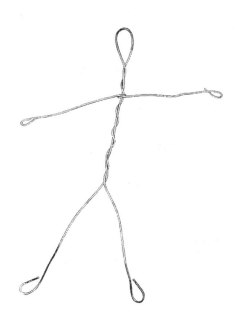

Method:
1. Take 1 piece of wire, cut to the size you wish to make your doll. The height will be approximately one-half the wire length. In other words, a 46 cm wire will make a doll about 23 cm tall, including the head. Fold the wire in half, making a small loop at the top. This will be used for attaching the head later. (Also used when making the soft sculptured head.)
2. Twist the wire below the loop into a body, leaving enough wire by the waist for legs. Make a small loop at the ends for the feet. (See drawings.)
3. Cut another wire to half the length of your first, and twist this around the body below the head, pulling each end of the wire out for the arms. Bend the ends into small circles or loops as you did for the feet.

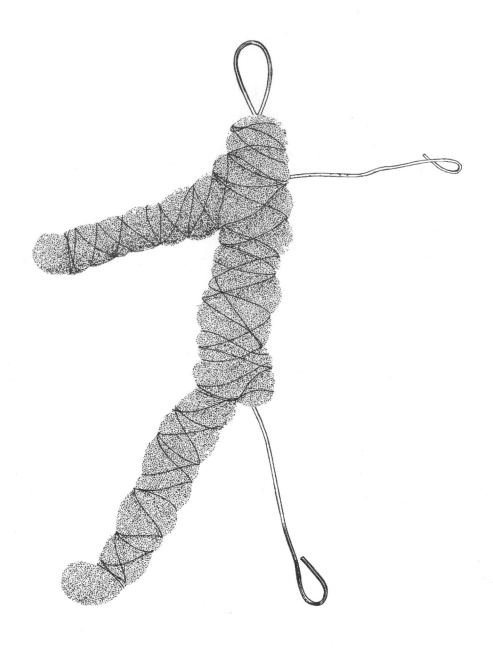

4. Now, taking small lengths or bits of the stuffing, begin to wrap this around the wire body, arms, and legs. Wrap small sections at a time, and tie with thread as you work.

5. The next step is to wrap strips of fabric or nylon stocking around the body to cover the padded frame. Cut strips about 4 cm wide. Start at the neck and wrap around the body, folding the strips where needed to fit the body. Join the strips as you work by taking a few small stitches through both the padding and the fabric.

6. Using pliers, carefully shape the feet into position and bend the hands a little as well.

7. You are now ready to add the head.a. In making Apple Heads, a wire is inserted into

the centre of the apple before the drying process. This wire is used to attach the Apple Head to the wire frame. See Apple Head doll instructions.

b. In making Nut Head dolls the pointed tip of the nut has to be sanded flat before the head can be attached. Keep sanding the point down until you see a tiny hole appear in the nut. A short piece of wire is inserted into this hole and glued in place. After the glue has hardened the Nut Head is attached to the wire loop at the top of the wire frame body by wrapping the head wire tightly around the body loop.

c. A purchased doll head comes with a wire already attached and is joined to the frame body in the same way as the other doll heads shown above. You may need to use a little masking tape to help hold the head firmly in place. This can be hidden with a strip of the body fabric. Spread glue around the lower end of the head before wrapping the body fabric over the wire join at the neck. Allow the glue to dry thoroughly.

8. Making and adding the hair:

a. It is necessary to make a little wig. Fun fur needs only to be cut to the size and shape you wish. Cut the wig a little larger than needed, and shape and fit it to suit the doll's face. Glue it to the top of the head first, and then shape. After shaping, continue to glue the wig in place around the head.

b. To make wig using yarn or wool, you need to cut a base from felt or fabric. Cut a small circle just large enough to cover the centre of the head. Cut the yarn long enough to reach from one shoulder up over the head and down to the other shoulder. You will need to cut 20 to 30 strands of yarn to cover the doll's head. (It will depend on the size of the head.) Lay the strands on the base so that they are centred. Make a seam along the centre from front to back joining the yarn to the base. The hair will be longer than you will likely want, but it will be cut to shape once the base has been glued to the head. Place glue on both the head and the underside of the wig, and press the wig to the top of the doll head. Cut and shape the hair to the style of your choice.

9. The next step will be to make the clothes and to dress the completed doll. By following the directions for making dresses, coats and pants discussed earlier, you should have no trouble designing and making interesting clothes for your wire frame dolls.

10. To make a stand for your doll, cut a piece of board or 12 mm plywood to the size and shape you wish. Decide the position on the board where you want to place the doll, and drill a hole using a 6 mm drill bit. Fit and glue a piece of 6 mm dowel into the hole. The dowel will need to be high enough to hold the doll upright but short enough to be hidden under the doll's clothing. I usually fit the dowel inside a pant leg or under a skirt.

11. By adding small items or props to the stands, you can make very interesting displays.

12 Apple Head Dolls

The fall or winter is the best time for making Apple Head dolls. Apples held over in storage for a long time are not as suited for this craft. In hot humid weather the apple will spoil before the drying process is completed. While an apple keeper and drier can be purchased in craft shops and used for making dried Apple Heads, we are using the early pioneer method. When making plans for your apple doll making, be sure to keep in mind that the Apple Heads shrink while drying. It is best to wait until the Apple Head is dry before making the wire frame body, or whatever body frame you plan to use for the completed doll. The measurements I gave in the wire frame instructions should be the approximate size needed for most dried Apple Heads.

Materials Needed:
1. A firm apple such as Delicious or MacIntosh.
2. A sharp paring knife.
3. Juice of one lemon and a small amount of salt.
4. 1 pipe cleaner or piece of fine wire.
5. White Glue.
6. Coloured beads or pins with heads or cloves can be used for making the eyes.
7. Cotton batting or stuffing, wool, yarn, fleece, or purchased fun fur can be used for making the wig hair.
8. Felt and fabric scraps, with matching sewing threads for making the clothing.
9. Adding little items, such as walking sticks and brooms, make the completed dolls more interesting.

Method:
1. Choose a fresh firm apple.
2. With a sharp paring knife, peel the skin off the apple as thinly as possible. Leave the stem at the top and the blossom at the lower end.
3. Carefully cut out where you want the eyes to be on the best side of the apple.
4. Cut out a small wedge between and slightly above the eyes for the forehead.

raw apple

5. Cut out a small wedge on each side of the nose area. Try to have the nose a little narrower at the bridge and wider at the bottom. All of the features will be quite large when you first carve the apple but keep in mind that these will shrink a great deal in the drying.

6. Below the nose, but leaving enough apple above the blossom for a chin, make the mouth. Carefully draw the tip of the knife along the apple being careful not to cut right into the apple. A slit is all that is needed. Remove a tiny bit of apple pulp left after drawing on the mouth with the knife.

7. The next step is to brush the salt over the apple face, and next brush the face with lemon juice. The pioneer and Indian apple dollmakers did not use this, but the Apple Head will get very dark in time if this is not done at the time of carving the face. Keep brushing the lemon juice over the apple face until all of the salt is melted and the apple is very wet.

8. Cut a pipe cleaner in half or use a short length of wire. Carefully push the wire down through the stem or top of the apple right through and out through the blossom end. (Remember, whatever you push into the apple will be held tightly in place and cannot be removed once the apple is dry.)

9. Make a bend in the lower end of the wire so that it cannot be pulled out of the apple. Next, make a hook at the top of the wire to use to hang the Apple Head up to dry.

10. Hang the head on a string or line in a warm dry place and allow the head to dry for three weeks. On the second or third day you may add the eyes or they can be added when the apple is dry. You can also dry the apples in a very slow oven set at 70 °C for a full 24 hours, either consecutively or spread out over two to three days. (That is, turning the oven on for approximately 8 hours and then turning it off until the next day and then turning it on again and so on.) There are several types of materials; (see making a wig in the Wire Frame instructions on page **No. 99**) which can be used for the wig.

Wool, yarn, fleece, cotton batting, or stuffing all make nice hair for Apple Head dolls, or fun fur can be used.

11. After making the wig, place glue on both the hair material and on the stem end or top of the apple and press the wig down firmly in place on the Apple Head. Allow to dry.

12. If you wish your Apple Head face to have colour, you can add it now, although the natural colour is more in keeping with the pioneer Apple Head dolls. The next step is to fasten the head to the body. We have used two methods for attaching the heads:

a. Push the wire at the lower end of the head down over the wire loop on the frame of the body and twist the two tightly together. Wrap a little masking tape over this join and cover with body fabric making a "neck" for the doll.

dry apple

b. Before making the wire frame body, push the two ends of the body wire down through the holes in a flat round button large enough so that the apple can rest on the top of the button, but not so large that it will show beyond the chin of the Apple Head.

You would then continue to make the body as previously described on page No. 97 in the wire frame body. Once the Apple Head is dried and wigged and ready to be added to the body, push the end wire down through one of the holes in the button and glue the head and the button together. This method makes a firm join and holds the head nicely in position. Cover the join and the button making a "neck" for the doll.

The Apple Head doll is now ready to be dressed. Following our directions for simple methods for making clothes for dolls you can design many interesting costumes for your Apple Head dolls. While I sew all of my doll clothes, you could glue the clothing to the doll's body if you wish. Just be sure that the glue is dry and held firmly in place as you work.

step 12b

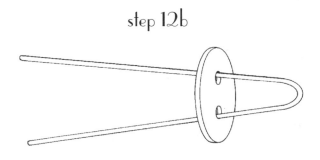

12 The Soft Sculptured Doll

Soft sculpturing means that you sculpt the shape of the facial features using a needle and thread. This doll is also made on a wire frame.

Materials Needed:
The same as for the wire frame dolls. However, you will need beads or glue-on eyes as well, and to be sure to have enough nylon stocking to completely cover the frame and the head.
Follow the steps for the wire frame doll through, and then continue with:

Method:
1. Wrap the loop with stuffing and add extra padding until you get the size of head you want.
2. Completely cover the frame and head with nylon stocking strips.
3. The shaping is done on the front of the padded head bringing any extra fullness or material to the back of the head.
4. Begin the stitching to create the facial features by working from the back of the head and using a stabbing type of stitching (pushing the needle in and out through the complete head thickness). Pull the thread tightly through to the back each time. Make sure that you hold the thread tight at the back as you do each stitch. There is no outline for the face. Use your imagination and create one. The work at the back of the head will look messy, but this is covered later.
5. Pad and shape the back of the head, adding more stuffing over the rough stitching. Sew a scrap of nylon stocking over the added stuffing, making a narrow seam along the crown of the head. The fun fur wig works well on this type of doll.

The completed doll is then dressed to suit the character which you have created.

104
104

13 Corn Husk Dolls

While corn husks which have been dried in the field in the fall can be used, and indeed were used by the Indian and pioneer dollmakers, most dollmakers today use the purchased husks sold in craft shops. A few scraps of cloth can be used to dress the doll if you wish, although the simpler corn dolls are often the most interesting. The doll we are making will be approximately 10 to 13 cm high.

Materials Needed:
1. Dried corn husks.
2. A small bead approximately 20 mm size.
3. Scissors and string.
4. Glycerine, (sold at the drug store), and dish detergent. Two capfuls of each, using the detergent bottle cap as a measure.
5. A large pail or pan half filled with warm water. (If you wish to have the husks a lighter shade, add a capful of laundry bleach.)
6. A heavy bath towel.
7. 1 pipe cleaner.
8. Wool or bits of yarn, or corn silk for the hair.

Method:
1. Place the corn husks in the pail half filled with warm water to which the glycerine and detergent, (bleach), have been added. Allow the husks to soak for about 20 to 30 minutes until they are very soft.
2. When the husks are soft, lay about 6 or 8 strips out on the bath towel. Trim off the tip of the husks and place the bead in the centre about half way down the length of the husks and to one side.
3. Carefully fold the husks down over the bead and bring the ends together neatly. Roll husks from one side around the bead and trim off any ends that may need to be cut off to shape the body of the doll.
4. Tie a piece of string around the husks below the bead and shape the husks to form a round head.

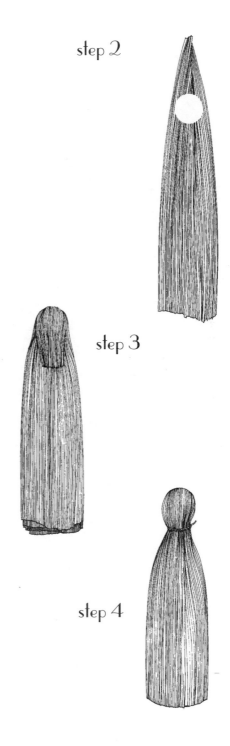

step 2

step 3

step 4

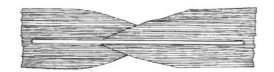

step 6

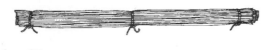

step 7

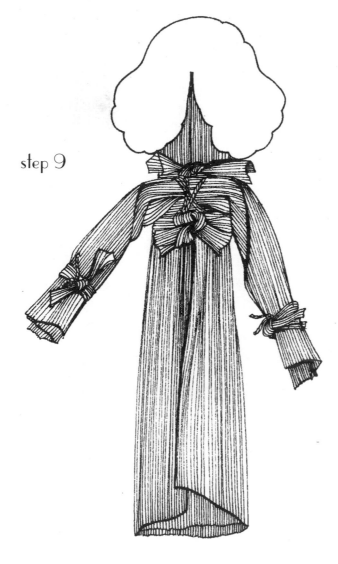

step 9

step 10

5. Next, shape the ends of the husks below the head and trim off the ends evenly and spread them out a little so that the doll can stand up.

6. Take one length of softened husk and lay it flat on the towel. Take a second husk and lay it on top of the first with the smaller end pointing toward the wide end of the first husk. Place the third husk directly on top as the first is laid and continue alternating the position for the next two husks.

7. Fold over the ends of the pipe cleaner just a little to shorten it. Lay the pipe cleaner lengthwise along one long side of this layer of husks and fold the husks over the ends of the wire so that the pipe cleaner ends are hidden.

8. Now roll and wrap the long layer of husks around the pipe cleaner starting at one long side. Tie the husks with string at the ends for hands. Tie again at the centre with a string that is 38 cm in length.

9. Place the centre tie at the centre back of the doll below the head. With the 38 cm string, tie the arms to the body, crossing the string over the body and arms in front and over again and tying at the back. Trim off any extra string.

10. Bring the arms to the front of the body and bend the pipe cleaner wire to the position you wish the arms to have.

11. Allow the doll to dry thoroughly before you add any trim or hair.

12. For the hair, you can fringe a few husks, or use yarn. Take several strands of yarn and lay and wrap them over the top of the husk doll's head. Tie them in place with a strand of coloured yarn, or use string and cover it with a strip of leather after you have tied it around the head. Shape the hair around the doll's head.

13. Scraps of cloth or leather can be used to cover the strings around the arms and body. I show several samples of corn husk dolls in our photographs, and from these you can create your own dolls.

14 Pop Up Puppet Dolls

At one time, dolls of very fine quality such as the bisque china head dolls we spoke of earlier, were made in puppets, or poupards, as they were called. Many of these poupard dolls had a music box, hidden by the dress, which played as the dolls were pushed up and down. Others had bells all around the clothing, which would ring as the dolls were worked. This type of puppet was usually only handled by an adult, who would be trying to entertain a child. But then, as we have also learned, dolls sometimes were really made for adults, and would only be passed down to a child after the grown-ups were no longer interested in them.

This doll, however, is quite easy to make. The puppet is worked up and down by pushing and pulling on the wooden stick or dowel.

Materials Needed:
1. A plastic bottle, such as a small bleach bottle one litre in size, without a handle.
2. Fancy wrapping paper or wallpaper to cover the bottle.
3. White glue.
4. A large wooden bead, about 38 mm in diameter with a hole in the centre.
5. A length of dowel to fit into the bead hole. A 12 mm dowel (1/2 inch) approximately 38 cm long.
6. Two bells and bits of trim.
7. A piece of cloth about 30 cm by 32 cm in size. Also scraps of felt for the hands and hat.
8. Paints or felt markers to mark on the face and hair.

Method:
1. Cut off the plastic bottle below the ridges at the top. Make a hole in the bottom large enough to allow the stick or dowel to move up and down freely.
2. Place the bottle on wrapping paper and trace around it. Trace a second circle 4 cm in diameter larger than the first circle. Cut out on this line and slash the circle to the inner line. Now glue the paper onto the bottom of the bottle and cut a hole in the paper at the opening for the stick.
3. Take another piece of wrapping paper and wrap it around the bottle to find out how much is needed. Cut, allowing enough to overlap. Make 2 cm slashes (cuts) into the paper all along one long end. Glue to the sides of the bottle, pressing the slashed edge over the bottom of the bottle so that the bottom is completely covered.
4. Glue the dowel into the hole in the bead and set aside to dry.
5. Paint the facial features and the hair on the bead. Let dry thoroughly.
6. Using the double fold method, cut out the shirt using the outline drawing as a guide. The width of 15 cm is along the fold at the top, while the centre fold will be the length, or 16 cm. Cut the arms 4.5 cm wide and the body 8 cm wide, remembering that the body will be 16 cm wide when opened out flat.
7. Turn the shirt right sides together and stitch along the underarm and body edges. Keep the seam quite narrow and even. Do the same on the other side.
8. With the shirt still turned inside out, make a small hem along the ends of the arms but do not stitch at this time.
9. Cut four pieces for the hands from felt using the pattern given in the drawing. Place two hand pieces together and, using

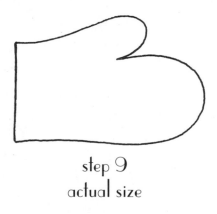

step 9
actual size

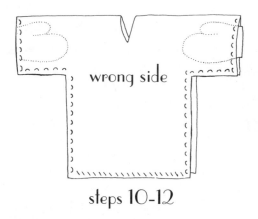

wrong side

steps 10-12

thread to match, sew them together using an overcast stitch. Leave the wrists open. Do the same to make the second hand. Stuff the hands with a little stuffing.

10. Follow the outline drawing showing the hands set inside the sleeves the thumbs pointing up. This will mean that the hands are inside the sleeves with the wrist ends along the edges of the sleeve openings. Stitch the hands and sleeve edges together right through all thicknesses.

11. Turn the shirt right side out, using a knitting needle to help push the sleeves and hands out. The hands should now be on the right side with the wrists sewn into the ends of the sleeves and the thumbs turned up.

12. Make a small slit at the centre neck edge at the fold just large enough to allow the dowel to pass through.

13. Slip the dowel with the painted head attached through the neck opening. Glue the shirt neck to the dowel as close to the head as possible. Allow the glue to dry. Then wrap a bit of cloth or trim around the neck and glue in place. Add a bow tie if you wish.

14. Push the dowel down through the hole in the lower end of the plastic bottle so that it comes down about 2 cm over the top of the cut-off bottle. Glue the shirt in place. Your doll is ready for you to add whatever trim you may wish to add.

15. Hat: Cut a circle a bit larger than the bead and from it, cut out a wedge as shown in the drawing. Overlap the cut edges and glue them in place. Glue the hat to the head of the puppet. Add a puff ball if you wish. Sew a loop or ring at the back of the shirt to hang up the puppet.

110

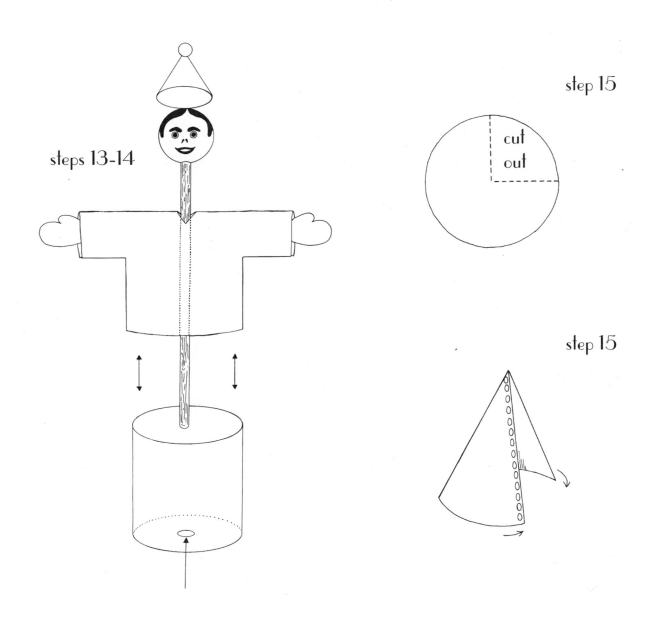

steps 13-14

step 15

cut
out

step 15

15 The Jumping Jack or Dancing Dan Dolls
Also known as "Limber Jack"

The wooden Jumping or Limber Jack, or Dancing Dan Dolls, are part of the heritage of every province. Most often, these were homemade from a scrap of wood, and made by the fathers and boys of the families.

Sometimes a travelling man would arrive a village and would either sell these dolls or put on a little show and give the dolls in return for food or lodging. In the days of early Canada, work was often seasonal and when times were difficult and money scarce, people turned to giving services in return for a meal or perhaps for another type of service.

The Jumping Jack dolls were popular with the boys and girls. However, because at that time it was not considered proper for boys to play with dolls, they would pretend to be entertaining the younger children of the family with the dolls. These young dollmakers were rather clever and could really make these dolls dance to a lively tune played on the harmonica by another lad.

The method of making the doll dance was to hold a flat, wooden slat between the knees. You would tap the slat or paddle with one hand. The other hand held the end of a long stick to which the doll was attached. You allowed the feet of the doll to touch the paddle. By tapping the paddle and making it jump, it would seem that the doll was dancing up and down. Of course, it was the movement of the paddle making the doll dance. These dolls are really quite simple to make.

Materials Needed:
1. A piece of pine 5 cm by 12 cm, and approximately 2 cm thick.
2. Scraps of 6 mm plywood for the arms and legs, or pine may be used in a 6 mm thickness (1/4 inch)
3. Tracing, and/or carbon paper to transfer the pattern.
4. Four common flat head nails 25 mm long (1 inch.)
5. Two 20 mm long cotter pins. (3/4 inch.)
6. One piece of 6 mm plywood cut to 15 cm by 50 cm for the paddle.
7. A 6 mm thick dowel 38 cm long. (1/4 inch dowel.)
8. A Fret or Coping saw.
9. A drill and a 3 mm (7/64") bit and 6 mm (1/4") bit.
10. Paints in colours of your choice for painting the facial features and the clothing on the completed doll. If you would rather not paint your doll you could draw on the features with a fine felt marker.
11. Sandpaper in a medium grain.

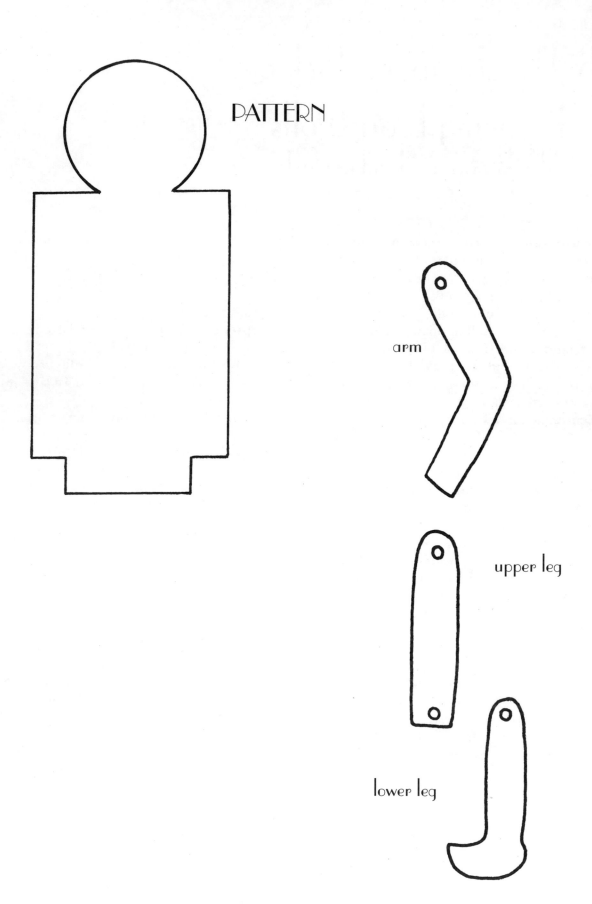

PATTERN

arm

upper leg

lower leg

114

Method:

1. After collecting all of the materials needed, trace the pattern on tissue paper and transfer to the piece of pine, and the scraps of plywood.

2. Following the pattern directions, cut out the head and hips with the fret saw. Sand rough edges.

3. Drill holes at the top and bottom of the upper legs and at the top of the lower legs. Also drill holes at the shoulder or top of the arms. All these holes should be drilled right through the wood. Use the 3 mm bit. (7164 inch).

4. Join the legs at the hip to the body with the nails and do the same with the arms to the shoulders. These joints should be free enough to allow the legs and arms to swing freely.

5. Join the upper and lower legs at the knee using the cotter pins. Insert the pins so that the open ends face each other on the inside of the legs. Spread the pins open to hold the pieces together but again be sure that the joint will swing freely.

6. Paint the doll to suit your own design or use the doll in the pattern and in the photo as a guide.

7. Sand and smooth all sides of the plywood paddle.

8. Using a 6 mm bit, (1/4 inch) drill a hole 1/3 of the way down from the top of the head at the back of the doll. Be careful not to drill more than halfway through the body thickness. Insert the stick or dowel. I do not glue the stick into the back of the doll because it is easier to carry the doll around or to sit it on a shelf without it. Should the dowel fit a little too tightly, sand it down a little with sandpaper.

Sit on the paddle and tap it at the centre to make it spring up and down. Hold the stick attached to the doll with your other hand and let the doll's feet rest on the paddle. Now dance!

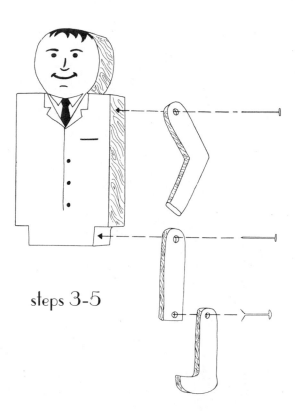

steps 3-5

16 How to make your first Rag Doll

If you can sew at all, then you can make a rag doll. While machine sewing will take less time, rag dolls can be sewn by hand.

Materials Needed:
1. Strong cotton - white, flesh colour or the colour of your choice. It should be 30 cm by 30 cm in size for the body. Sugar bags that have been bleached make lovely rag dolls. Try to find a cotton fabric the colour of your own skin to make the doll like you. I use many shades to make my multicultural dolls more realistic of the people they represent.
2. Dressmaker's tracing or carbon paper, and paper to trace the pattern on. Also a sharp, soft lead pencil.
3. Thread to match the doll's body, or white thread, and colours to match any fabrics for the clothes which you are using.
4. Polyester stuffing. 500 grams of stuffing can be purchased in a bag at fabric and craft shops.
5. A long, pointed knitting needle. This is to turn things inside out and to push out the points and curves, as well as to push the stuffing in place.
6. A popsicle stick or a coffee stick.
7. Embroidery threads for the eyes, nose and mouth. You may use felt markers or embroidery paints or scraps of felt for the face, if you prefer. (Sometimes the markers spread or run on the fabric. Test them on a scrap of fabric first.)
8. Yarn for the hair, or a piece of fake fur for a wig. It should be 20 cm by 15 cm. If using yarn you will need a large ball of about 50 grams.
9. Narrow ribbon to tie the hair braids.
10. Fabric for the dress in colour and print of your choice approximately 30 cm long, of fabric that is 90 cm in width.
11. Scraps of felt for shoes.
12. Embroidery and sewing needles as well as a large-eyed darning needle.
13. Scissors.

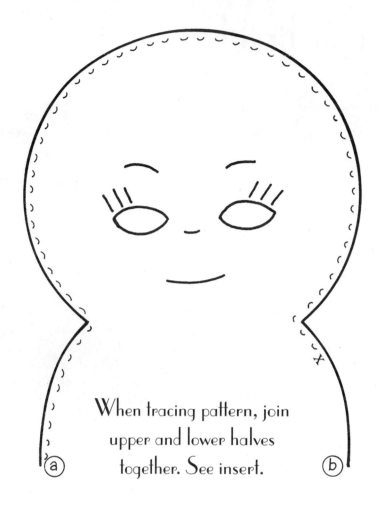

When tracing pattern, join upper and lower halves together. See insert.

(a)   (b)

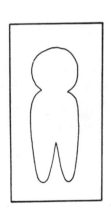

When you have collected all of these things, you will find it helpful to place all of the supplies on a tray or in the lid of a box. Be sure to keep these away from small children. Following the pattern outlines, trace the pattern onto strong white or brown paper and cut out. Paper bags are good for this.

Method:

1. Lay the pattern for the body and arms on top of two thicknesses of the body fabric. Pin the body pattern to the fabric with dressmaker's pins.

2. Lay carbon paper or dressmaker's tracing paper between the fabric and the pattern for the head. (The rest of the pattern is already pinned to the fabric.) Trace the face onto the body fabric. Remove the tracing paper, and pin the head pattern onto the fabric.

3. Cut around the body and arm pattern pieces being sure to cut through both thicknesses of the cloth. You need four pieces for the arms, so cut two sets.

4. Remove the pins and the pattern. Keep the pattern handy to study for any markings which may be needed later.

5. At this point do the face. You can make this by using embroidery thread, embroidery paints, or felt markers. If using paints, be sure that they are dry before you continue with the doll. Felt scraps can also be used. They can be sewn or glued to the doll's face.

6. Placing the right sides together (the face is on the right side), pin the fabric body pieces together.

7. Stitch from the X marked on the pattern around to the small x. *Leave the rest of the side seam open.*

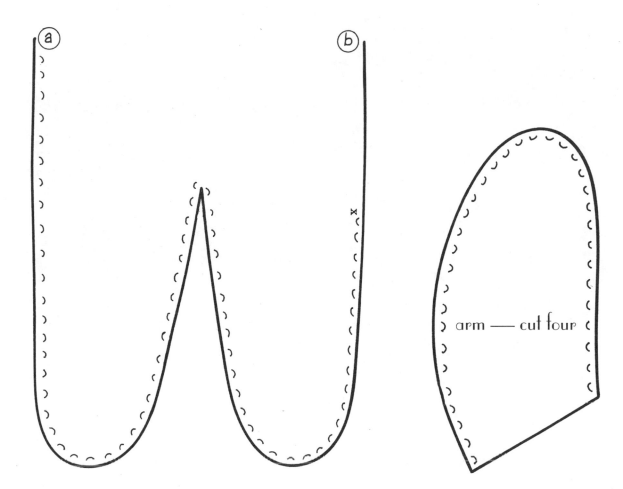

arm — cut four

8. See photo and the markings on the pattern stitched in black. Use this as a guide. Stitch the arms as well, *leaving the straight ends open* in order to be able to turn them right side out and to stuff.

9. Using the scissors, clip very carefully around the rounded shapes of the doll, being sure not to clip right into the stitching. Also clip at the neck and between the legs. This will avoid the material puckering when you turn it right side out.

10. Now turn the doll right side out through the small opening left at the side. Do the same with the arms. Here is the time to use the knitting needle. Be very gentle, but make the head and body nicely shaped.

11. Now, taking small handfuls of the stuffing, begin to stuff the doll through the opening. Do the legs first, pushing the stuffing firmly into place with the knitting needle. *Stuff the doll firmly.* After the legs are stuffed, begin to stuff the head. Shape the head as you work and when it is stuffed to the nose, insert a small coffee stir stick or wooden stick into the head and neck area. This will help keep the doll's head from falling all about after the doll has been played with for some time. Continue stuffing, working and padding all around the stick and down the body until the doll is firm.

12. Pin the body opening closed and using a strong thread, finish sewing up the body with an overcast stitch. Go over this seam several times and then fasten the thread off.

13. Stuff the arms again using the knitting needle. When they are nicely shaped, turn in the raw edges and pin the arms to the body. (See photo.) Sew the arms to the body as you did the opening, making sure that they are sewn firmly in place. Go over all joins several times.

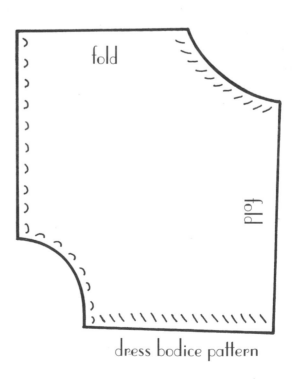

fold

fold

dress bodice pattern

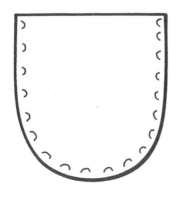

shoe pattern —
cut four

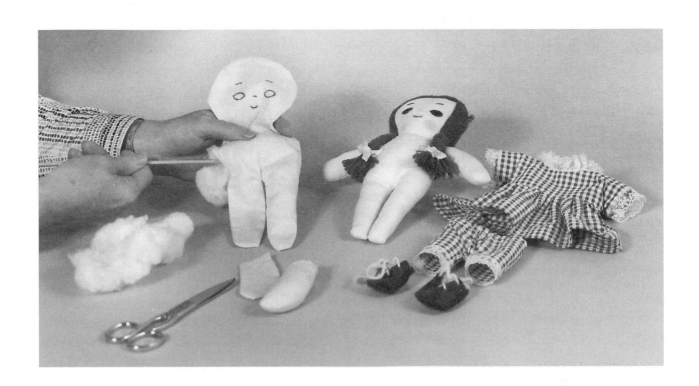

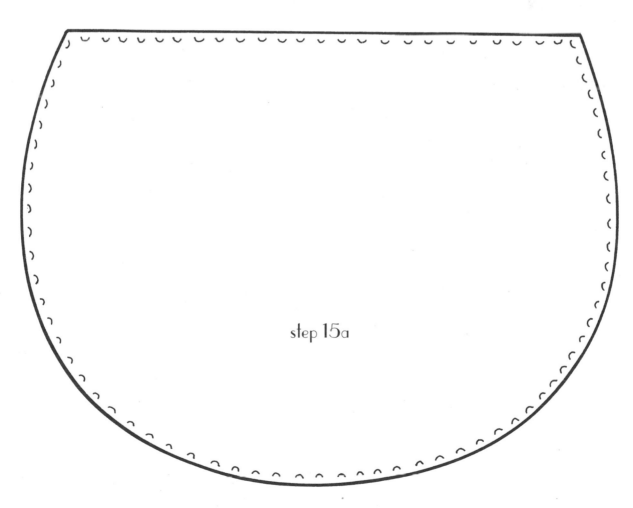

step 15a

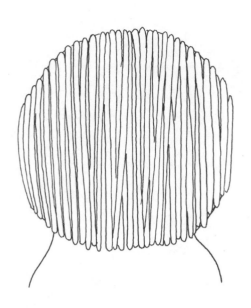
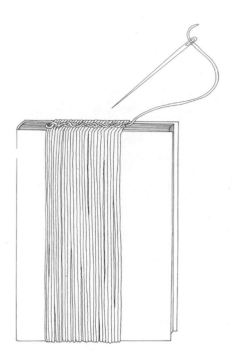

14. Take a ball-point pen and sign the back of the doll with your name or initials and the date! That's right! You can even number your dolls if you like. I sign mine … MH/97 or whatever the year is. Your trade mark is something to be proud of.

15. Hair:

a. For the wig, trace the pattern on to paper and then pin the pattern to the wrong side of the fun fur. Cut the wig to shape with sharp scissors. Remove the pattern and brush out any of the shedding hairs from the fresh cut. Next, using a matching coloured thread, run a gathering stitch by hand all around the outer edge of the wig. Gently begin to pull the gathers up loosely. Leaving the needle threaded, put the wig on the doll's head and pin in place. Continue to pull up the gathering and shape the wig to the head. Fasten off the thread so that it will not work loose. Using a double thread of the same shade, sew the wig in place, working from below the ear area around to the front and down the side and around the back, shaping all the while until completely sewn. Again fasten securely and cut off remaining thread.

b. To make hair from wool or yarn:

b1. Using a large-eyed darning needle and yarn, tie a knot at the end and begin to work back and forth with the yarn across the back of the head.

b2. Take a small stitch through the back at the neck edge and draw the yarn across the head to the front seam along the top of the head. Work back by again taking a small stitch at the front and drawing the yarn back down to the neck edge. Work in this way until the back of the head is pretty well filled in with the yarn hairs.

b3. Once the back of the head is covered in this way, we can now make the wool or yarn wig. Following the drawings, wind the yarn around the long side of a book 23 cm x 33 cm x 3 cm in size, about 30 or 40 times, keeping the yarn firm and tight (but not so tight that you pull the book out of shape).

b4. Next, thread a darning needle with a very long strand of yarn and starting

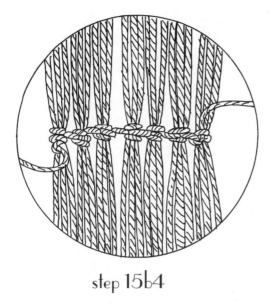

step 15b4

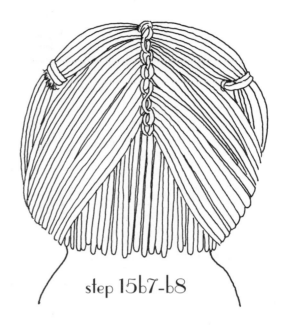

step 15b7-b8

along the narrow edge (3 cm), sew the strands together, two at a time. Make little knots as you go. Work towards the front and then back again. Leave the needle threaded.

b5. Take the scissors and cut the yarn from the book at the opposite narrow edge (3 cm). Now you will have two long sides hanging down from the centre stitching or sewing. Try to keep each strand on its own side of the centre seam.

b6. Starting at the centre seam, begin to pin the wig in place, keeping the seam in line with the doll's nose. Pin straight across the centre seam, gently pulling the wig to down the back of the head but not separating the hairs too much.

b7. Take the threaded needle and begin to sew the wig to the doll's head, stitching right through the stuffing and out again. Back stitch as you work until the centre is firmly sewn to the head. Now carefully pull the hair around and along the head to the ear area, holding it in place with pins.

b8. Thread the needle again with yarn and push it from the front right through to the back, at the neck below the ear area. Leave a long piece of yarn at both ends of that stitch. Cut the needle from the yarn and wrap this long strand of yarn from the front around the hair, being sure that the hair is smooth as you work. Tie the hair firmly to the neck. Do the same on each side, and again on each side of the centre part above the eyes to hold the hair in place around the face.

b9. You can leave the hair as is or braid it and tie it with ribbons. If tying it, tie it first with the yarn, and then tie the ribbons around the braids.

16. Follow the pattern given here or make up one of your own for the clothes.

Bodice:

Lay the bodice on a double fold and cut in one piece. Then slit the bodice up the centre back. Sew a small hem around the neck and down the back openings on both sides. Trim neck with lace or trim of your choice. Do arm hems in the same way. Pin right sides together and sew small seams under arms and down

step 15b9

side seam. If fabric frays, zigzag or overcast seams. Turn right side out and press.

Skirt:

Cut a strip of the dress fabric, 60 cm wide by 13.5 cm deep. Sew the two 13.5 cm ends together right sides facing, leaving a waist opening about 5 cm from the top of the seam. Hem along each side of the waist opening, stitching across the top of the seam. Press seam open flat. Turn skirt right side out. Run a gathering thread around the top of the skirt. Pull thread up to make the skirt fit the waist edge of the bodice. Fasten gathering thread firmly and cut off. The bodice lower waist edge and the skirt waist edge should now be the same size. Make a narrow hem along the lower edge of the skirt approximately 2 cm deep.

Turn the skirt wrong side out. Place the bodice inside the skirt with the right side of the bodice and the right side of the skirt facing. Pin the two together all around the waist. When you are sure that they are nicely fitted, baste and sew the seam with a small running stitch. (To baste means to use a long running stitch.) Turn the dress right side out and put on the doll. You can sew snap fasteners on the back opening, or hand sew up the back of the dress.

Shoes:

If you want your doll to have shoes, trace the pattern on paper, pin this to a double thickness of coloured felt, and cut out. (You need four shoe pieces to make a pair.) Taking two pieces, sew all around the sides and toe, leaving the top open. Be sure to tie firm knots at the start and finish of this seam. Cut out a very small "V" from the front of each shoe. Thread white yarn across the "V" using a darning needle. The yarn becomes the shoe laces. Put shoes on doll and tie the laces in a neat bow.

Underpants:

If you want underpants for your rag doll, follow the instructions in How to Make Pants using the folded tube method. (*See p. 75*)

124

Doll and Photograph Credits

Unless otherwise indicated, the dolls are in the collection of the institution or individual providing the photographs.

photo: Ron Rochon

page 46 — Bedroom or Boudoir Doll: Cherry Aitken; photo: Rick Packham

page 47 — Russian Matroshka Dolls: Author's collection; photo: Ron Rochon

page 48,49 — Dolls by John Halfyard: Aileen Devereux; photo: Ruth Jacobsen. Special thanks to *Westworld Magazine*, Vancouver, B.C.

page 50, 51 — Dolls by Betsy Howard. Courtenay and District Museum, by permission of Mrs. Kath Kirk; photo: Rick Packham. Research: Mary Slemin

page 52 — Shelly Fowler's Pedlar Doll: Shelly Fowler

page 53 — Dolls from Line Desjardins: Line Desjardins; photo: Ron Craib

page 54 — Eaton Beauty Doll: Archives, Eaton's of Canada

page 55 — Dolls of Wendy Gibbs: Wendy Gibbs

page 56 — Elizabeth Nind and Applecraft: Elizabeth Nind.

Instructions for Making Them: All the dolls in this section are in the author's collection and were photographed under her direction, with the exception of:

page 58 — Rolled Rag Dolls: Ruth Keene; photo: Ron Rochon. By permission of The Grange, Art Gallery of Ontario

page 104, 107 — Corn Husk Dolls: McCord Museum, McGill University

Front Cover Photograph: Students of Cassandra Public School, Don Mills, Ontario, with the author. Used by permission of the principal. Photo: George Bettson